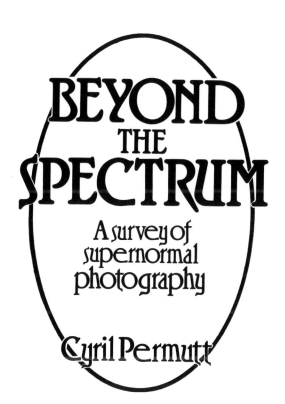

BEYOND
THE
SPECTRUM

A survey of
supernormal
photography

Cyril Permutt

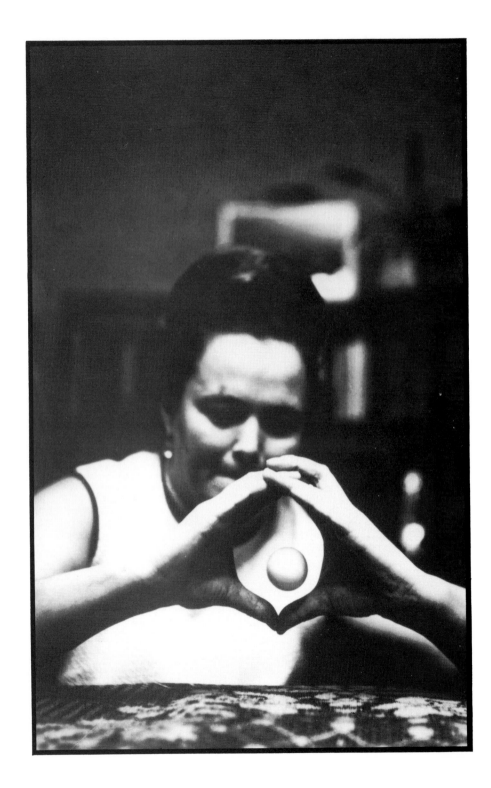

BEYOND THE SPECTRUM

A survey of supernormal photography

Cyril Permutt

 Patrick Stephens, Cambridge

Dedication
To my dear wife Sadie
and our children
Philip
Elaine and Richard
Pamela and Jeffrey,
and to Rachel and Melanie
to whom the future belongs.

First published in 1983

Front endpaper *Ectoplasmic drapery appeared on this*
photograph taken at a Mrs Meurig Morris appearance in
South Africa by a Cape Times *newspaper photographer in*
1935.
Frontispiece *Nina Kulagina demonstrating her amazing*
psychokinetic ability (courtesy of the Souvenir Press Ltd).

British Library Cataloguing in Publication Data

Permutt, Cyril
  Beyond the spectrum.
  1. Spirit photography
  I. Title
  778.9'91331   BF1381

  ISBN 0-85059-620-3

Photoset in 10 on 11 pt Plantin by Manuset Limited,
Baldock, Herts. Printed in Great Britain on 115 gsm
Fineblade coated cartridge by R.J. Acford Ltd,
Chichester, and bound by Norton-Bridge Bookbinders
Ltd, Stotfold, Herts, for the publishers, Patrick Stephens
Limited, Bar Hill, Cambridge, CB3 8EL, England.

Contents

Introduction

Beyond The Spectrum was written as a result of the convergence of my researches into the history of photography and my enquiries into the supernormal. I found that beneath the layers of accidentally produced semi-transparent ghost-like figures, double exposures, processing errors, and deliberate fraud that have accumulated since the earliest years of photography, when the photographic process itself was shrouded in mystery and often referred to as a black art, there remains a solid core of inexplicable supernormal photographs.

Supernormal photographs can be divided into two main groups—those which record visible supernormal phenomena and those which are the result of direct action of supernormal influences on the sensitive film or paper itself. Each of these groups can be further subdivided into spontaneous examples which occur without the intervention of the observer and those which are arranged as a controlled experiment. All four types of photographs are equally valid proofs of supernormal phenomena.

Most of mankind's supernormal talents are by definition non-physical and so are difficult to demonstrate, but the end product of supernormal photography is a physical record which cannot be denied. Although sceptics will always cite cases of fraud the answer to that is, once again, simply to try it yourself. When you have controlled the process personally you know for certain that the phenomena which have been produced are authentic. If enough people can be encouraged to conduct such experiments, then we may be able to help bridge the gap between the spontaneous occurrences of supernormal phenomena and the scientific researches now being conducted which seem to inhibit the very talents which they are trying to examine.

Perhaps because of the methods then in use most of the supernormal photographs taken during the Victorian era were 'spirit photographs'. However, modern photographic processes can be extended to produce more than their usual thin slices of reality and can be made to show pictures of the past, of extra spectra and dimensions and, perhaps, even of the future. The evidence now being accumulated as proof of

Opposite *The ghost of Raynam Hall, September 19 1936. Neither the negative from which this photograph was taken, nor the print itself, have been touched up or tampered with in any way before being reproduced here. The photographer, Captain H.C. Provand, a Director of Indre Shira Ltd, Court Photographers, declared: 'I am unable to offer any explanation about the ghost picture. At the time of the exposure I saw nothing!'*

Psychic photograph by Letty Hyde who died on November 1 1921. This photograph, with William Hope and Mrs Buxton as mediums, was taken in September 1924.

the existence of the supernormal calls for a reappraisal of the part played by talents such as psychokinesis and telepathy in the production of supernormal photographs and for further experimenting in all the allied fields of both the mental and physical aspects of the supernormal.

Like the interest in stereoscopic photography, the public's interest in supernormal photography has waxed and waned peaking in about 25 or 30-year cycles, and we are now entering into another period of intense interest. The first such period was in the 1860s and '70s and another occurred after the First World War and was exemplified by the setting up of the Society for the Study of Supernormal Pictures which was active from 1919 to 1923. The present excitement about supernormal photography is based on two advances in photography itself. The first is the explosion of interest in photography in general which has meant that almost everyone owns or has access to a camera and so can now experiment for themselves, and the second is the perfecting of the modern in-camera processing of film as the very nature of the film packs used in the Polaroid and Kodak instant print cameras precludes fraudulent manipulation of the film. In a letter to Curtis Fuller, President of the Illinois Society for Psychic Research quoted by Jule Eisenbud MD in his book *The World of Ted Serios*, Mr Stanford Calderwood, Vice-President of the Polaroid Corporation, says, 'Let me stress that while a clever man could tamper in advance with our film, I know of no way that he could do it if you were to show up with the film you bought in a store at random and watched him load and shoot. Tampering with the film would be a long and complicated procedure and nothing that could be done by sleight of hand, especially if he had to photograph two or three pictures (or thoughts) on the same roll without re-loading the camera and without an opportunity to substitute something in front of or behind the lens'.

I have tried as far as is possible to avoid becoming involved too deeply here with the concept of personal survival after death or to go into details of the many other forms of human mental interaction with physical matter, but if, as I believe has been shown, mental power and concentration can stop a clock or start one which has been broken, move crockery across a table, bend metal and set a compass needle spinning, then it is reasonable to assume that it must be able to affect the delicate sensitive surface of a photographic emulsion.

Acknowledgements

I acknowledge with pleasure the encouragement, expert advice and sometimes criticism that I have received from so many good friends. It would need another book to list their names but I thank them all and in particular I extend my grateful thanks to those who have sent me supernormal or psychic photographs in the past and to the many more who I hope will do so in the future.

I also extend my grateful thanks to the publishers and authors who granted me permission to mention and quote from their books and publications and allowed me to use their photographs.

I would like to thank especially Miss Eleanor O'Keeffe, secretary of the Society for Psychical Research, Tony Ortzen, editor of *The Psychic News*, B.E.C. Howarth-Loomes, Brian Coe, Curator of the Kodak Museum, and Messrs Kodak Limited for their many kindnesses, although it must be understood that mentioning Messrs Kodak Limited is not meant to imply their approval or verification of anything shown or written here—though they did suggest that we use as much Kodak film as possible.

Finally, let me add that this book would not be complete without acknowledging the debts that I owe to my dear wife, Sadie, for her unfailing support, to our daughter, Elaine, for the way in which she so gracefully excelled in the roles of researcher and secretary, to our sons, Jeffrey and Philip, and our cousin, Ian Cipin, for their help with research and photography, and also to Philip for acting as my scientific advisor.

Above *Lady and Sir Arthur Conan Doyle, Dr Abraham Wallace, James Coates and other members of the Society for the Study of Supernormal Pictures. This photograph, taken by William Hope, also has an extra psychic image of an unidentified man.*

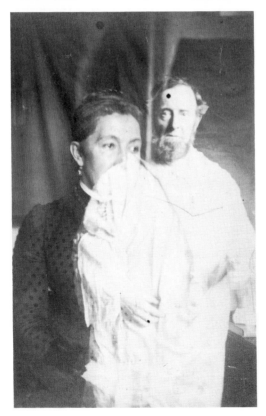

Left *'Taken in my room with my own camera and plate by Mr Eglinton and developed directly afterwards in my presence December 9 1886.' Signed Mary Burchett.*

Chapter 1

Psychic photography

The supernormal exists beside us, here and now! Only now in the 1980s we can at long last prove that the miracles, prophesying and magic that are found in the religious beliefs of mankind are based on fact. Supernormal photography shows that the wonderful experiences described by prophets and believers of all faiths are true.

Everyone is amazed when they first see a photograph with a supernormal extra image but research and experiment have proved that many people can and do produce them. Those illustrated here are only a few of the large number of attested and authenticated supernormal photographs which I could have selected from my files which prove conclusively that there is more to life than we perceive with our gross physical senses and which show how photographic processes can capture the images of other dimensions and other times.

The physical miracles of the past would today be thought of as examples of psychokinesis. Prophecy would be termed clairvoyance or precognition, and the healing once claimed as the province of religious leaders and magicians is now more commonly seen as the spirit healing which helps so many people today. These supernormal phenomena are examples of the psychic extentions of mankind and before we could photograph them we had to take them on trust with faith as our only guide.

Photography has provided us with an exciting method of recording and investigating those supernormal talents of mankind which were so deeply smothered in superstition in the past that it is only now, in the last quarter of the 20th century, that scientific investigations are really being directed towards them.

Supernormal photography is as old as photography itself but when the first photographers found inexplicable extra images in their work they thought that they might have been caused by some unknown variables in the wonderful new chemicals and apparatus that they were using.

When the invention of photography was first announced in January 1839 it was not possible to take portraits of people. Both the silvered plates of the daguerreotype, invented by Louis Mandé Daguerre in France, and the sensitised paper negatives of the photogenic drawings invented by William Henry Fox Talbot in England, needed exposures of half an hour or more which made portraiture impossible and it was not until further improvements in cameras, lenses, photographic chemicals and processes reduced the exposure times to a few seconds that portraiture became practical.

Interest in Spiritualism had been rising since the Fox sisters of Hydesville, New

York, had begun to give demonstrations of psychic phenomena in 1848 but no photographs are available from that time because, although Antoine Claudet had taken indoor portraits at night using an oxy-hydrogen light in London as early as 1840, night time or indoor photography was not really practical until Bengal lights, fireworks burned in a glass lantern and giving off a bright blue/white light, came into use in 1858.

In those days the photographer had first to prepare a glass plate by coating it with a film of collodion (gun cotton dissolved in ether) containing iodide of potassium, sensitise it by dipping it into a bath of nitrate of silver and then take the photograph whilst the plate was still wet. Each exposure was exciting, each batch of chemicals was a new experiment and every unusual result a stimulant. W. Campbell of Jersey City USA became the first man to take a supernormal photograph. At the twentieth meeting of the American Photographic Society in 1860 he showed a test photograph that he had taken of an empty chair, there had been no one else in the studio when he had made the exposure but, when the plate was developed, the picture of a small boy appeared in the chair. Campbell was not able to produce any more photographs of this nature, however, and it was not until the following year that the history of supernormal photography really began.

On October 5 1861, in a photographic studio at 258 Washington Street, Boston, USA, William H. Mumler, an enthusiastic and experienced amateur photographer, was developing some experimental self-portraits which he had taken, when the ghostly figure of a young woman appeared next to him in one of the pictures and he recognised her as a cousin who had passed away 12 years earlier. He recalled that whilst he was posing for that particular picture he had experienced a most peculiar trembling sensation in his right arm which left him feeling almost exhausted. The photograph attracted great interest and was investigated by both Spiritualists and some of the most prominent photographers of the day, who came to accept the fact that as Mumler had stated 'This photograph was taken by myself of myself and there was not a living soul in the room beside myself'. Mumler was soon overwhelmed by public demand for his spirit photographs and, beginning by taking two hours a day from his regular work as the principal engraver for Bigelow Bros and Kennard one of Bostons best jewellers, he soon had to give up his job entirely and devote himself to psychic photography.

William Black, a leading Boston portrait photographer who was known internationally as the inventor of the acid nitrate bath (an important improvement in the photographic process), was one of a number of professional photographers who investigated Mumler's methods. Attending a sitting at Mumler's studio Black carefully examined camera, plate, dipper and bath, and had his eye on the plate from the moment its preparation began until it was sensitised and locked in the dark slide. After his portrait was taken Black removed it from the camera and took it into the darkroom himself where, as it was developed, the figure of a man was seen leaning on his shoulder. Mumler described himself as a 'medium for taking spirit photographs' and although the psychic extras he obtained were often unrecognisable and blurred, in many cases they were distinct likenesses of deceased friends and relatives of the sitters. By this time the news of Mumler's ability to take psychic photographs had spread all over North America and had aroused great interest in Great Britain and Europe. Sets of 12 of his psychic photographs were sold for $5 in the United States and packets of three for 3/6d in England.

Although he had never been interested in spirits or Spiritualism, Mumler became

Photograph of a woman with the extra spirit image of her late sister. A 1905 photograph of the sister is included for comparison.

the centre of great controversy. Even the testimony of US Court of Appeals Judge John Edmonds—who had gone to test Mumler certain that he was a trickster and had left convinced that Mumler had actually produced psychic photographs under test conditions—failed to quieten the critics and disbelievers and Mumler finally moved to New York where, in 1869, he was charging as much as $10 a photograph. His studio was frequented by some of the most eminent people in the land and, although many of the pictures which he produced were undistinguished, on one occasion at least he produced a recognisable and astonishing psychic portrait of Abraham Lincoln. A lady heavily veiled and wearing a black dress had given her name as Mrs Tydall when she called unannounced at his studio and asked to be photographed. In his own words, 'I requested her to be seated, went into my darkroom and coated a plate. When I came out I found her seated with a veil still over her face. The crepe veil was so thick it was impossible to distinguish a single feature of her face. I asked if she intended having her picture taken with her veil. She replied, "When you are ready, I will remove it". I said I was ready, upon which she removed the veil and the picture was taken'. It was only when he saw the print that he realised that his sitter had been Mrs Lincoln. 'The picture of Mr Lincoln is an excellent one. He is seen standing behind her, with his hands resting on her shoulders, and looking down with a pleasant smile.'

In 1863 Dr Child of Philadelphia reported that he found Mumler very willing to give him every opportunity of investigating the matter and, as he said, earnest himself to find a rational solution to the mystery. He permitted him to watch all his operations in the darkroom and out of it and allowed him to examine all his apparatus. Dr Child showed the pictures made at that time, while he and several

Left *This photograph of President Lincoln's widow was William H. Mumler's most famous photograph. Although Mumler did not know at the time that his sitter was Mrs Lincoln, the spirit form of the assassinated President and their late son appeared behind her in the photograph.*

Right *Moses A. Dow and spirit, photograph by Mumler, Boston, USA.*

Right *Portrait of C.H. Foster with spirit of Adah Issacs Menkin, by William Mumler.*

friends were watching the whole process, from the plate cleaning to the fixing. He took the precaution to mark each plate with a diamond before it was used. Yet on each was a spirit image, and he failed completely to discover any human agency concerned in the formation of the spirit picture. As to these, they differed very considerably from any that he had ever seen, and he knew of no way of imitating them.

The extras shown on Mumler's photographs did not, however, meet with universal acclaim and, after much controversy, pressure from the Mayor of New York led to his being arrested and charged with fraud but the testimony of eminent New Yorkers, including the famous Broadway photographer Jeremiah Gurney who affirmed that as a professional photographer of 28 years experience he had witnessed Mumler's process, scrutinised everything, and could find nothing which savoured of fraud or trickery, led to Mumler being exonerated and the case being dismissed by Judge Dowling who presided over the court.

In a letter about supernormal photography in *The Spiritual Magazine* Vol IV, No 2, February 1863, Benjamin Coleman told of another early psychic photographer. 'Dr Gardner the pioneer of Spiritualism in Boston first heard that some pictures had been taken in Roxbury which had a second figure that could not be accounted for by the operator. Soon after this event the Roxbury photographer heard that similar pictures were being produced by Mr Mumler, in Boston, which were called spirit pictures, and being a very decided orthodox Christian he refused to have any more pictures made that bore the second figure saying that if it had anything to do

A spirit photograph obtained through the mediumship of Frederick Hudson. The sitter was Mr Raby Wootton who was advised to visit Hudson during a seance at his home. Mr Wootton and his friends took the photograph and developed it themselves without allowing Hudson to take any part in the manipulations.

with Spiritualism it was the work of the Devil, and he would no longer lend himself to it. Dr Gardner, however, found by closer enquiry that a young man in the employ of the Roxbury artist was a medium, and the doctor induced this young man, despite of his employer's scruples, to give him a private sitting at which . . . the doctor's likeness and a remarkable spirit figure was obtained.'

Other photographers, both amateur and professional, who had the ability to produce inexplicable extra images on photographs came forward in Great Britain and Europe as well as in the United States. The first and most famous of those in England was Frederick Hudson, who was brought to the public's attention by Mrs Samuel Guppy one of the best known British Spiritualist mediums of the time. Her husband was an enthusiastic amateur photographer who had made many unsuccessful attempts to obtain spirit photographs. In March 1872 Mr and Mrs Guppy visited Frederick Hudson's photographic studio at Palmers Terrace, Holloway Road, London, to have their photographs taken and during the proceedings Samuel Guppy suggested an interesting experiment. 'I directed Mr Hudson how to arrange the drapery forming the background and requested my wife to sit behind it while I was being taken. While so sitting, and Mr Hudson preparing the plate, a wreath of artificial flowers was placed on my head suddenly. There were some artificial flowers about, and they had been put on a table in one picture taken of my wife, but there was no wreath. Mr Hudson was in his darkroom, and my wife behind the drapery at the time. No other person was present. The picture taken shows a white figure standing behind me, like a person covered with a sheet.' Other spirit photographs followed, the affirmed condition necessary was that of the presence of a medium. Hudson went on to become the best known British psychic photographer and was known for producing supernormal extras on his plates under the closest of scrutiny.

John Beattie, a prominent professional photographer who had been experimenting with psychic photography with some success for over a year, gave details in *The British Journal of Photography*, July 11 1873, of a series of experiments which he had conducted with Frederick Hudson in which Hudson's daughter had sat as the medium. At that time Hudson was charging one guinea to make his experiments but only on the understanding that he would not be blamed if nothing unusual appeared, which often was the case. Beattie described how, with a friend, he had examined most scrupulously the glass room in Hudson's garden in which the experiments were to take place, the operating room with its yellow light and procelain baths, the 10 × 8-inch camera with its 6-inch lens and all the machinery involved. He also maintained that he had marked the photographic plate to be used and had watched it being both coated and prepared.

For the first photograph which Hudson took, giving an exposure of about a minute, Beattie sat as the subject in profile to the background and Hudson's daughter acting as the medium stood next to him, but no extra appeared. In the next experiment Beattie reported: 'All was the same except that the medium sat behind the background. On the picture being developed a sitting figure beside myself came out in front of me and between the background and myself. I am sitting in profile in the picture: the figure is in three-quarter position—in front of me, but altogether between me and the background. The figure is draped in black, with a white coloured plaid over the head, and is like both a brother and nephew of mine. This last point I do not press, because the face is like that of a dead person and is underlighted.

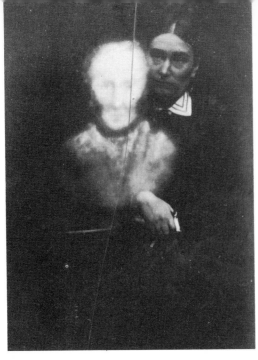

Left *Mrs Collins and the image of her husband's late father. A photograph obtained by Mr Parkes 1875.*

Right *The medium Florence Cook who produced the materialised form of Katie King.*

'In my last trial—all, if possible, being more strictly attended to than before, and in the same place relative to me—there came out a standing female figure, clothed in a black skirt, and having a white-coloured, thin linen drapery something like a shawl pattern, upon her shoulders, over which a profuse mass of black hair loosely hung. The figure is in front of me, and, as it were, partially between me and the camera.'

He goes on to say: 'If the figures standing by me in the pictures were not produced as I have suggested (remember their possibility has been otherwise proved), I do not know how they were there; but I must state a few ways by which they were *not* made. They were not made by double exposure, nor by figures being projected in space in any way; they were not the result of mirrors; they were not produced by any machinery in the background, behind it, above it, or below it, nor by any contrivance connected with the bath, the camera or the camera slide.'

Although as with all supernormal phenomena the possibility of fraud must always be guarded against, psychic extras have been produced under the strictest of controlled conditions again and again, the medium not being allowed near the camera, plates, film or processing and, indeed, sometimes with the medium in an adjoining room whilst the entire experiment was taking place. Mr Parkes, another well known photographer who produced psychic extras, is reported in the *Christian Spiritualist*, January 1875, to have had an aperture made in the wall of his darkroom so that he could be watched whilst preparing and processing the plates. Parkes often worked in the evening taking many psychic photographs by means of a magnesium light.

Several mediums in England during the early 1870s had the ability to materialise spirit forms and faces during their seances which were similar in appearance to those produced in psychic photographs. At this type of materialising seance, which originated in the United States, the medium was usually tied securely to a chair and often screened wholly or partly by curtains. On many occasions witnesses held the medium's hands or arms as an extra precaution and at some of these seances the materialised face spoke to those present. Miss Florence Cook, a celebrated material-ising medium, was thoroughly investigated in 1874 by Sir William Crookes—

President of the Royal Society, inventor of the cathode ray tube and one of the greatest scientists of his time—who recorded details of seances in 1874 in which five complete sets of photographic apparatus consisting of one whole plate, one half plate, one quarter plate and two binocular stereoscopic cameras were used to photograph the medium and the form of a spirit known as Katie King who was materialised by her. The face of Katie King had begun to materialise during seances with Florence Cook some time earlier and before Katie King had appeared for the last time at the end of May 1874 she had materialised completely on many occasions and had even walked around the room. Photographs taken during these seances show Florence Cook in a trance together with the materialised Katie King and others show Katie standing arm in arm with Sir William Crookes himself. Unless one is prepared to accept the unlikely assumption that this brilliant scientist was either a dupe or a deliberate fraud and that the many outstanding scientists and professional people who acted as his assistants and witnesses at these seances were completely hoodwinked by a simple young girl, there can be no doubt about the authenticity of these photographs.

The mediumship of Florence Cook was investigated by many other independent observers who included mediums, newspaper reporters, Spiritualists, scientists and eminent laymen. In her book *There is no Death* Florence Marryat, who attended many of Florence Cook's demonstrations, gives a detailed eye witness account of various physical phenomena which came through her. She tells of being present on many occasions when the spirit form of Katie King was materialised and photographed whilst Florence Cook was looking on and of having seen both Katie King and Florence Cook together on several occasions. She also relates how the materialised physical form of Katie King varied in height, size and looks from time to time, sometimes appearing as a small, slight brunette much like Florence Cook and, at the other extreme, sometimes appearing as a large buxom blonde with a white skin and a profusion of golden red hair.

The great upsurge of interest in Spiritualism and psychic phenomena in general led to the founding of the Society for Psychical Research in London in 1882, 'to examine without prejudice or prepossession and in a scientific spirit those faculties

Left *Taken by magnesium light during a seance, this photograph by William Crookes shows both Florence Cook (the entranced medium) and the materialising form of Katie King.*

Below *William Crookes' famous photograph of the phantom form of Katie King materialising beside her medium Florence Cook, seen seated on the right. Surgeon James M. Gully, seated on the left, checked the pulse rate of the materialisation and testified that it was different to that of the entranced medium.*

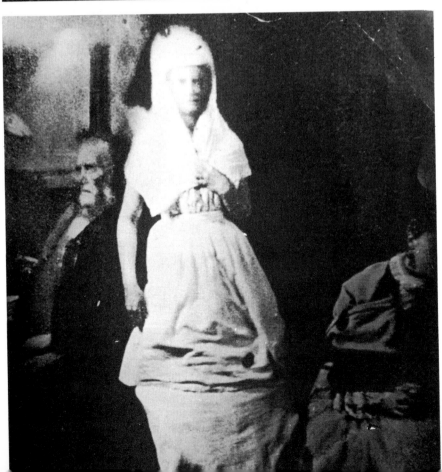

of men, real or supposed, which appear to be inexplicable on any generally recognised hypothesis'. The American society that was founded in 1885 became a branch of the British society but was re-established as the American Society for Psychical Research Inc in 1905. However, neither of these societies became greatly involved with psychic photography. One paper by Mrs Henry Sidgwick, wife of Professor Henry Sidgwick the President of the London Society, 'On Spirit Photographs, a Reply to Mr A.R. Wallace' published in the *Proceedings of The Society for Psychic Research*, Vol III, 1891, pp 268-89, was apparently written without any personal investigation or experimenting at all and after accusing almost everyone concerned with fraud went on to say, 'It appeared to me that after eliminating what might certainly or probably be attributed to trickery, the remaining evidence was hardly sufficient in amount to establish even a *prima facie* case for investigation, in view of the immense theoretical difficulties involved'.

Theoretical difficulties there may have been but the society was even then investigating other supernormal phenomena such as levitation, telekinesis and poltergeist activity all of which also involve direct mental influence on an object or physical process and which are no less difficult to explain theoretically. Many people, it seems, would rather believe the most involved and unlikely tales of deception and fraud than accept the simple fact that on rare occasions extra images are formed by the photographic processes which cannot be explained by the normal action of light on a sensitised photographic emulsion.

There were indeed some frauds and opportunists involved in psychic photography, as there are in all walks of life. M. Baguet, a well known French photographer who was in London for a time, was convicted in Paris in 1875 after confessing that he had tampered with photographs to produce extra images on occasions when he was unable to produce real psychic photographs but, even so, evidence was given at his trial of the many genuine psychic photographs that he had taken. The ability to take psychic photographs is no guarantee of a person's honesty and there seems to be no doubt that Baguet cheated on many occasions but this does not alter the fact that supernormal photographs of many different kinds have been produced under exacting test conditions where no fraud was possible.

Fake spirit photographs are easy to produce. For the first few years after the invention of photography exposures took so long that people often moved into or out of a scene which was being photographed and thus showed up as partly-exposed semi-transparent figures and this led to the idea of 'ghost' photographs. The first mention of such 'supernormal' pictures was made by Sir David Brewster in his book *The Stereoscope* published by John Murray in London in 1856. In an article in *The Scientific Review*, August 1 1866, Sir David Brewster recalled that the idea of these phantom photographs first came to him when he saw a calotype photograph of York Minster taken by the famous photographers Hill and Adamson in 1844. A lad who had been sitting on a step near the doorway had apparently got up and left about half way through the exposure and so appeared transparent in the finished photograph. 'The value and application of this fact did not at first present itself to me, but after I had contrived the lenticular stereoscope I saw that such transparent pictures might be used for various purposes (of entertainment).' Ghost and spirit photographs and stereographs were being sold commercially in the 1850s and 1860s but they were sold as a parlour novelty and no attempt was made to present them as genuine psychic photographs.

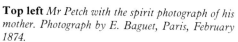

Top left *Mr Petch with the spirit photograph of his mother. Photograph by E. Baguet, Paris, February 1874.*

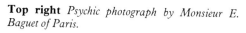

Top right *Psychic photograph by Monsieur E. Baguet of Paris.*

Left *William Hope's portrait of Mrs Longcake and the psychic image of her deceased sister in law.*

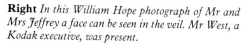

Right *In this William Hope photograph of Mr and Mrs Jeffrey a face can be seen in the veil. Mr West, a Kodak executive, was present.*

There were many other methods by which it was suggested trick photographs could have been produced. It was said that prepared plates or cut films might have been used or even substituted by slight of hand for fresh ones provided by investigators. Alternatively an assistant could show his face through the curtained background during the exposure or, perhaps, quinine sulphate or similar fluorescent materials that are invisible to the human eye but record on the photographic emulsion could have been used to paint an image on the background. However, it is stretching the bounds of possibility too far to suggest that tricks such as these could have fooled the professional photographers, scientists and other critical observers who have on many occasions witnessed and supervised the production of psychic photographs.

The effect of the expectations of the experimenters on the results obtained has been seen in many fields of scientific research and in one study of such cases, *Pygmalion in the Classroom: Teacher Expectation and Pupils' Intellectual Development*, New York and London 1968, Robert Rosenthal and Lenore Jacobson enlarge on the tendency of an expectation to be 'a self-fulfilling prophecy'. They tell how, when laboratory rats have been divided into two groups chosen at random and labelled 'maze-bright' and 'maze-dull' respectively, experimenters influenced by these labels found that the 'maze-bright' rats produced significantly better results in mazes than the other group, whilst in another experiment when the teachers of a group of school children who had been chosen at random were told that this group were due to have an intellectual spurt it was found that a number of them did in fact make a significantly greater gain in their IQ than their classmates. In both these cases it was only the experimenters' expectation of success that influenced the result and it has been found that this influence can work in both directions causing either a positive or negative result dependent upon the investigators' attitude to the experiment.

It is very often the investigators' own preconceived opinions about psychic photography which prevents them from achieving any positive results themselves, or even from being willing to recognise or admit such results when they are achieved by others and, indeed, this has at times led to the most ridiculous theories and explanations being prepared to avoid the acceptance of the fact that inexplicable psychic images and extras have been produced time after time in circumstances that preclude any normal photographic explanation. This is born out in an article entitled 'The Effect of the Experimenters' Attitude in Parapsychology' by Robert H. Thouless in *The Journal of the Society for Psychical Research*, March 1976, where after going into the subject in some detail he discusses an experimental investigation into out-of-body experiences undertaken by K. Osis and Boneita Perskari which strongly suggests, 'that it was the experimenters' lack of interest in positive scoring . . . that was effective in preventing such scoring . . .'.

A solid mass of supernormal photographs which, although apparently inexplicable, are nevertheless authentic and consist of photographs taken and witnessed by people of unimpeachable honesty for whom no personal gain is involved and in circumstances that rule out any question of fraud or deceit has been slowly accumulated. These show that many different supernormal effects have been produced on photographic emulsions and the theory that they are often produced or at least controlled either consciously or subsconsciously by the human mind is reinforced by the fact that the earliest supernormal photographs reflected the then current rise of interest in Spiritualism. Typical was the cloud like effect so common

Mr and Mrs Buxton and their young son photographed near Exmouth in 1924 by William Hope. The face of their elder son, who had died in 1923, is seen above Mrs Buxton who is almost concealed by the cloud of ectoplasm which extends at the side of the dead boy's face to form a replica of the head of his white pony which had died a little before he had. The face that can be seen on Mr Buxton's waistcoat was that of his brother who had also died in 1923.

in such pictures which seems like a screen on to which the picture is projected and the muslin-like drapery seen around many of the psychic extras was typical of the very effects expected by the experimenters.

Supernormal photographs vary enormously from simple fogging, patches, bars or streamers of light, exposures over part of or the whole surface of the plate or film (including the rebates that are covered up in the camera), negatives that have been exposed normally and yet when processed bear no image at all and provide all black or all white prints, negatives or prints on which inexplicable images appear or disappear some time after they are processed, through an entire range of extras and anomalies up to recognisable images of persons or objects which are non-physical or which were not present when the plate or film was exposed.

Many of the series of supernormal photographs which were produced over a period of several years by Mrs Marguerite Du Pont Lee were psychic photographs of a Dr Bocock, an Episcopalian minister who had been dead for ten years, and others were direct thoughtographs, yet they failed to convince sceptics who insisted that she must be a charlatan and a fraud in spite of the fact that, as Professor James H. Hyslop of Columbia University carefully pointed out in his account of these experiments in an article 'Some Unusual Phenomena in Photography' published in the *Proceedings of the American Society for Psychical Research* part 3, Vol VIII, 1914, the very wealthy Mrs Lee was one of the millionare Du Ponts who not only was not in need of any money but who had gone to great lengths to avoid any notoriety or publicity at all.

Supernormal photographs have been made by almost all the photographic processes from the wet-plate to X-ray and Polaroid films. William Hope's first psychic photograph was made on a tintype plate. He was 37 years old when he took a portrait of a friend one sunny Sunday afternoon in 1905 using the tintype plate

which gave a direct positive image on its metal surface and, after the plate was developed, he was astonished to see what at first appeared to be a white flare become a picture of his friend's sister who had died many years earlier. Soon after this happened, Hope went to a Spiritualist meeting in Crewe where a Mrs Buxton, who was there with her husband, was told that she had an undeveloped talent and would become a medium herself. Hope introduced himself to Mr and Mrs Buxton and told them of the photograph that he had taken and, together with five friends, they formed a group which became famous as the Crewe Circle. Although the Circle conducted all kinds of Spiritualist and supernormal experiments their main success was with the production of psychic photographs and, as it became obvious that the extras were only produced in the photographs when both William Hope and Mrs Buxton were present, the others gradually stopped attending leaving Hope and Mrs Buxton to carry on working together until Hope died 28 years later in 1933.

The psychic photographs produced by this combination drew world wide attention and the honesty of their methods and authenticity of their results were investigated and attested to by many eminent people. Archdeacon Colley of the Anglican Church, a well known psychic researcher, gave them many searching tests in the early days of the Crew Circle, finally presenting them with a new quarter plate camera as a sign of his conviction of the worth of their work and, in 1910, William Walker, President of the Buxton Camera Club, wrote them a two-page testimonial recording that 'psychic extras or spirit photographs' were obtained under test conditions and strict attention to detail laid down by Mr Walker who had 35 years experience of photography and over 25 years as an investigator of Spiritualism.

J. Malcolm Bird, associate editor of the *Scientific American*, who visited England in 1922 to investigate the position of Spiritualism and psychic photography, was not a Spiritualist himself and had an impartial approach to the subject. In the series of articles which he wrote for the *Scientific American* and in his book *My Psychic Adventures*, published by Allen and Unwin Ltd in 1923, he gives details of his sittings with Hope and Mrs Buxton which clearly show his sceptical and analytical approach to the subject. He tells of his purchase of photographic plates at the

Left *Issued by the Society for the Study of Supernormal Pictures with Budget No 97 in 1923, this postcard shows both a photograph of the boy taken whilst he was living and his psychic image which appeared on the photograph taken of his parents after his death.*

Right *A rare psychic photograph of an Asian couple by William Hope. The extra image was recognised as a deceased member of their family.*

Westminster Photographic Exchange in Victoria St, which he picked out at random from the classified telephone directory and confirms that the plates were not out of his possession nor out of his sight at any time. He comments on the bareness of the small studio and adjoining darkroom at the British College of Psychic Science where the experiments took place. Hope was a carpenter and Bird gives his opinion that neither Hope nor Mrs Buxton, whom he likened in appearance and mentality to a charwoman, had sufficient acumen or intelligence to conduct any elaborate fraud or deceit, an opinion incidentally which has been agreed with by many people to whom I have spoken who knew both Hope and Mrs Buxton personally.

Bird tells of the controlled test conditions which he imposed, how he examined the premises, camera and lens, and how two photographs were taken on plates which he personally chose at random from the sealed package in his possession and which he himself developed after the exposures. The first of these—a portrait of himself and Sir Arthur Conan Doyle who had accompanied him—was a perfectly ordinary photograph but the second—a portrait of Bird on his own—to his amazement showed two distinct extras one of which was a clear image of a human face.

Sir Arthur Conan Doyle was an honorary officer of the Society for the Study of Supernormal Pictures, a group composed mainly of professional photographers who spent much time in the 1920s investigating all aspects of supernormal photography. Intrigued by the unwanted extra images which often spoiled their photographs, they made a thorough investigation of the subject and produced an amazing series of photographs which compared the spirit photographs with those which had been taken of the same persons whilst they were living.

The meetings between Professor Fukurai and William Hope, which occurred in 1928 when the former came to England to attend the International Spiritualist Federation, were of great importance to supernormal photography and both of the experiments which they conducted together gave excellent results. At the first of these experiments, on September 19 1928, Fukurai and a Japanese friend, Kenichi Yamamoto, bought a sealed packet of six quarter-plates in London and took it with them to Hope's home where the experiments were to take place.

The sealed packet of plates was placed in the centre of a table and Fukurai, Yamamoto, Hope and his assistant Mrs Buxton made a circle around the table by holding each other's hands. Then accompanied by Yamamoto and Hope, Fukurai took the package of plates into the darkroom where he opened the sealed packet under a red light, removed two of the plates, signed them and loaded them into a dark slide, put the remaining plates into a cardboard box and put the box into his pocket for safe keeping. They all went straight to Hope's studio at the back of his house where Fukurai examined the camera and lens most carefully and placed the dark slide in the camera, opened its lid and sat on a chair in front of the camera. Hope, placing his left hand on Mrs Buxton, removed the lens cap with his right, and with his right hand pressed to his forehead concentrated throughout the ten-second exposure. Yamamoto stood next to Hope and watched him carefully all the time. The second plate was exposed in the same way, Hope touching only the lens cap.

Fukurai returned to the darkroom with the slide and exchanged the plates for two new ones from the packet in his pocket. Again he signed them before loading them into the slide and two more photographs were then taken in the same way. Then, taking the four exposed plates into the darkroom, he put them into a developing tank and watched carefully as Hope poured the developing solution over them. As they developed it became apparent that the first two only had photographs of Fukurai but the second two both showed, in addition to his portrait, the extra photograph of a European woman and other unclear images.

Fukurai used the remaining two plates for an experiment in his own speciality, thoughtography. Holding them together between his hands he asked Hope to concentrate on them, which he did by putting his hands over Fukurai's for five or six seconds. Fukurai immediately developed them and although one of them was blank the other shows an image like a distorted smoke ring which resembles that on one of the psychic photographs that they had just taken.

The second of these experiments took place on September 29 1928. Once again Fukurai and Yamamoto called at Hope's house taking with them a packet of six quarter plates that they had purchased in London and two photographs were taken with Hope again doing nothing except to remove and replace the lens cap of the camera. They were developed immediately, the first showed only Fukurai but the second had, in addition, the portrait of a man and, although Hope knew no French, the words 'Je connais ce monsieur' appeared above the extra image.

The experiment in thoughtography which followed again produced a most interesting and significant result. In the darkroom Fukurai took three new plates from the packet in his pocket and, signing his name on them in Japanese and holding them in a pile between his hands, asked Hope to concentrate on the middle plate of the sandwich. He explained that Japanese mediums had achieved good results in experiments of this nature. Hope had not tried anything like this before but, after concentrating for five or six minutes, said that he might have managed to produce something on one of the other plates too. Fukurai developed the three plates at the same time, the bottom one was blank but the centre plate had two images one on the inner part and one on the edge, whilst the top plate had an image on one edge. The image on the inner part of the centre plate was a group of flowers but the amazing part of this experiment was the fact that the incomplete image on the edge of the centre plate lined up with the similarly incomplete image on the edge of the top plate and, when matched together, they formed the image of a

Portrait of Professor T. Fukurai with psychic extra and message 'Je connais ce monsieur' taken by William Hope on September 29 1928.

Major C.H. Mowbray and friend. This photograph with the recognised and identified extra male image was produced by William Hope under the most stringently controlled conditions (courtesy of Mrs Simmons).

complete plant. Fukurai had intended to conduct just such an experiment to produce two halves of a picture on two separate plates at a third meeting with Hope but, although he wrote asking for another experiment to be tried, circumstances prevented their meeting again and Fukurai remained convinced that somehow the fact that Hope would not be able to arrange a third set of experiments had caused the two halves of a picture to be produced on two separate plates at their second and last meeting.

Major C.H. Mowbray, author of *Transition* published by LSA Publications Ltd, London, in 1936, which contains the records and photographs of some of the psychic phenomena, apports, ectoplasmic materialisations and levitations that he had witnessed and which he put forward as evidence of life after death, wrote an account in *Light*, December 26 1935, the quarterly magazine of the College of Psychic Science Ltd, of a sitting which he had had with William Hope. The result was a photograph of a dead child called Penanne.

'I only had one sitting with William Hope, of Crewe, the photographic medium, but I was completely satisfied with the result.

'Having arranged an appointment, I asked "Penanne's" mother if she would care to come with me. She was delighted at the idea, so we two went off to Crewe together. Hope only expected me to come by myself; and, to the day of his passing, he had no idea who my companion was.

'I had previously bought a packet of Imperial extra-rapid quarter-plates from a dealer in Old Bond Street, and had amused myself the night before by making marks on the outside of the unopened wrapper, so that I could easily distinguish them in a bad light.

'Having gone round to Hope's house we found he was out—not having expected me that day, but he soon returned and the sitting started. Hope, Mrs Buxton (who used to work with him), my friend and I sat round a table in full sunlight with the unopened packet of plates in the middle. After a few minutes, I was told to take up the plates and hold them with one hand on top and the other underneath. Hope placed his hands on mine, my friend placing her hands on Hope's and finally Mrs

One of a series of psychic photographs taken by William Hope in the strict test conditions supervised by William Walker, President of the Buxton Camera Club.

Buxton did the same, thus there were four hands on top and four underneath the packet.

'After we had held the packet this way for five minutes or so, Hope said it would do, and he told me to come with him into the darkroom. I placed the plates in my pocket and followed him; but before doing anything else, I made a most careful examination of the dark slide he handed to me, and I satisfied myself that it was quite normal.

'I then went into the darkroom with him, opened the packet of plates (which was the one I had bought in London), took out two from the middle, inserted them in the slide, signed them, placed the remaining ten plates in my pocket and, holding the slide in my hand, went into the "studio"—a small greenhouse with an army blanket stretched over a brick wall which served as a background.

'I examined all this most carefully to make sure that no one could get behind the blanket and poke his head through (an explanation which an exceedingly well known scientist gave me later as to how the extra had come on the plate).

'Sitters with Hope will remember how he worked with an old Lancaster "Instant-ograph" without shutter or cap, and this I was allowed almost to pull to pieces to see if I could discover anything unusual about it. Except for its age it was quite normal.

'My friend and I sat down and Hope proceeded to focus us; I got up and focused the camera myself, Hope taking my place; and I then inserted the slide in the camera, sat down again in front of it, and he made the exposure by drawing the slide, keeping it up for ten seconds or so, and then pushing it down again. I got up, reversed the slide and Hope made a second exposure in the same way. I then removed the slide from the camera, went with Hope to the darkroom, put the two plates into the developer together, covered the dish with a card to prevent light getting on them (the darkroom used, like the camera, being somewhat ramshackle) and developed them myself, Hope at no time interfering with me. After fixing, I found there was an "extra" on the plate, the other being normal.

'When I received the print, I found the "extra" to be the photograph of a man in civilian clothing, extremely like an ancestor of my friend, only younger. She told me that his name was M—.

'After lunch, we went back for the second sitting—the procedure being exactly the same as before, except for the holding of the plates, which of course, had remained in my possession all the time. Two plates were exposed, which, on development by myself, were found to have an "extra" on each, these were of "Penanne". How do I know they were the child's photographs?

'Because both her parents recognised her, and surely they should know their own child. I have the mother's letter before me as I write. She says: "My husband and I are absolutely certain, without a shadow of doubt, that the "extras" on the two photographs are "Penanne", as she looked the last three months before she passed out".

'On talking it over with her later, she told me that she knew it was the child because; 1) it is exactly like her; 2) three days before her passing she had an operation which necessitated her hair on the right side of her head being shaved off: this shaving can be seen on the photograph; 3) she had a slight cast in one eye—this also can be observed.

'No photograph was taken of the child after the side of her head was shaved. She never recovered from the operation.

This psychic photograph, taken by Boursnell in 1895, has an extra image of a young coloured boy. The sitter was J.H. Evans.

'Surely this is proof enough of identity—many people have suffered the death penalty on less evidence.

'When we were on the point of leaving, Mrs Buxton asked if we would like to try to get a skotograph; so we came back. I slipped a plate into a slide which she held against her head for a few seconds. On developing, I found a curious ribbon-marking on the plate.

'In spite of what some people have said against William Hope, I give it as my considered opinion that these are genuine "extras" and I say deliberately that not only did he not trick, but that he had no chance of doing so. And, even if I were entirely bluffed, how could he have got a non-existent photo of "Penanne" with the shaven hair to put on a plate? I am convinced that either these were photos of the actual child or else photos of thought forms in the mother's mind, but if the latter, why didn't Hope get them until the second sitting? My friend wanted an "extra" of "Penanne"—that's really what she had gone to Crewe for—and the last person she had in mind was this ancestor of hers. I think this might dispose of the thought of the telepathic idea.

David Daguid, the Glasgow trance and photographic medium, with psychic extra of an old Scotsman. Photograph taken by Boursnell.

'I have gone into detail in this case to answer before hand many objections that may be raised.'

There were many other photographers who had produced authenticated psychic photographs by this time. They ranged from mediums like R. Boursnell, who was a professional photographer in London for most of this period—of whom James Coates in his book *Photographing the Invisible* published in London by L.N. Fowler and Co, and in Chicago, USA, by The Advanced Thought Publishing Co. in 1911 recounts, 'Before Mumler got his first picture in 1861, Boursnell got curious appearances on his plates, not only spoiling them, but leading to disagreements with his employer who accused him of not cleaning the glass properly',—to Edward Wyllie, another medium-photographer who was instrumental in producing psychic photographs in Los Angeles, California, USA, at the turn of the century with investigators who used their own cameras to expose plates that they provided and developed themselves.

H. Blackwell, who had been experimenting with psychic photography for many years, was also an admirer of Boursnell's work. In an article entitled 'Spirit Photo-

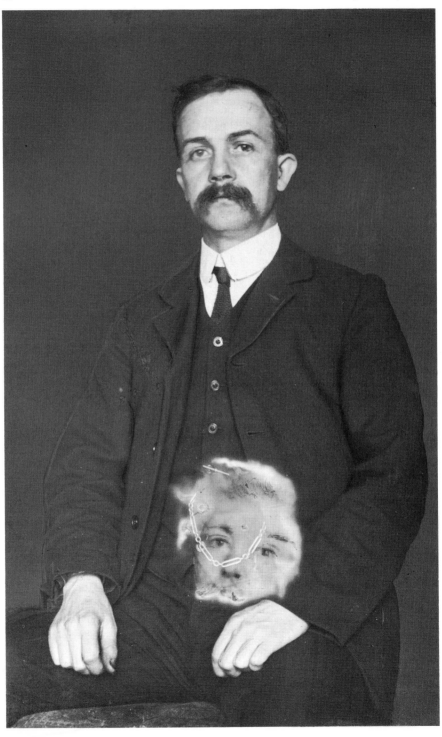

Left *Robert Whiteford, a professional photographer of Rothesay, provided the plate, supervised the 16-second exposure, and developed the plate himself when this portrait of him with an unidentified psychic extra was taken by Edward Wyllie on October 9 1909.*

Above *Mr Alexander Dallachy of Rothesay and the spirit image of his twin brother Robert. Photograph by Edward Wyllie 1909.*

graphs' in *The London Magazine*, written in 1910 when Boursnell was nearly 80 years old and had retired, Blackwell wrote:

'In my many sittings with him, extending over a period of ten years not because of any personal doubt, but to make the evidence of more value, a fresh packet of plates had been taken each time, initialled and dated usually, placed in the slides, the camera examined and, with but few exceptions the plates have been developed immediately. Several friends have done the same including one editor of an important London newspaper, who wrote a long and interesting article on his experience.

'Having made a close study of the subject, both here and in America, aided by a very large collection of psychic photographs, and being an amateur photographer, I am fully convinced that Mr Boursnell is absolutely honourable and worthy of the utmost respect.'

After telling how Boursnell had always shrunk from publicity and declined the greater number of his would-be sitters, although he had been for some 15 years the only medium in England or all of Europe who could usually be depended upon to produce successful psychic photographs, Blackwell included many examples of psychic photographs taken by Boursnell and others including a photograph of Dr Theordore Hansmann with a psychic portrait of his father on it. Dr Hansmann, who was then the oldest physician in Washington, had psychic gifts himself and this photograph, which was his own work, was part of his collection of spirit photographs which was described as the finest in the world.

The emergence of modern science in the early part of the 19th century had helped to dispel the superstitions of the past, but scientists could not relate the evidence obtained by psychic photography to the progress that they were making in material fields. Because of this most of the research into supernormal photography was carried on by Spiritualists who believed that the psychic photographs that they produced were clear proof of post mortem survival. However, it has now become generally realised that the ability to photograph an invisible or even a non-material object is no more improbable than the original discovery of the latent image itself. In the last decade the scientific attitude towards all aspects of the supernormal has undergone a radical change and the existence of a non-physical element in life has been accepted, even though most psychic and supernormal photographs involve apparent infringements of scientific assumptions. Evidence of a common ground between psychic phenomena and modern physics is growing and the time is rapidly approaching when they will come together and explain just how supernormal photographs are produced.

Chapter 2

Photographing physical phenomena

Psychic phenomena have occurred throughout the history of mankind. Socrates and Joan of Arc both heard prophetic voices and had previsions of the future, the Old and New Testaments have many accounts of similar phenomena. Auras, levitation and prophecying, like the well recorded phenomena associated with St Francis of Assisi, St Theresa, St Helena, St Alphonso of Liguori and St Joseph of Copertino (1603-1663), have been attributed to many saintly people. These stories are probably not entirely true, but neither are they entirely lies or fiction. Before they were written down the emotions and fallible human memories of those concerned may well have taken a hand and coloured the accounts of the incidents. The most probable account is the story of St Joseph of Copertino, who was beatified in 1753. It is recorded that his levitation was witnessed not only by the people and members of his order but also on one occasion by Pope Urban VIII himself. Think how wonderful it would be if we had a photographic record of the miracles and mysteries recorded in the holy books of the great religions and how it would affect our lives and our religious observance!

We now have a great advantage over those few of our ancestors who witnessed these great events and it is that, since the invention of photography in 1839, we have been able to make a record of this type of event and the added impact of moving pictures and video tape recorders emphasises this advantage.

The scientific investigation of psychic phenomena in Great Britain really commenced with the investigations of men of the stature of Alfred Russell Wallace, whose genius anticipated much of Charles Darwin's work, and other members of the Dialectic Society of London in the 1860s who included many well known scientists of the day, 36 of whom met in January 1869 to study mediumistic phenomena scientifically. These investigations confirmed many of the reported phenomena produced during seances and led to William Crookes becoming involved in the speculation that was going on about the cause or causes of these manifestations and to his experiments with two of the most powerful mediums then available, Florence Cook and Daniel Dunglas Home. The eventual result of all this was the establishment, in 1882, of the Society for Psychical Research. Many outstanding physical mediums were discovered and investigated during the next three or four decades and many respected scientists reported and photographed their psychokinetic feats.

The ability of mediums such as Eusapia Palladino, Martha Béraud, Stanislawa Tomczyk and Kate Goligher to produce levitation, materialisations and movements

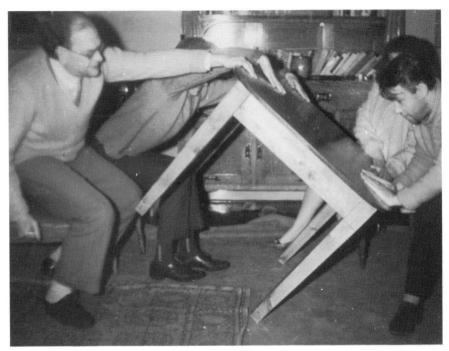

PK table-tilting experiment photographed in complete darkness using infra-red flash by K. Batcheldor, seen at front left operating the rubber bulb of the camera remote shutter control.

without physical contact was established beyond doubt but no real explanation of their talents was brought forward.

Effects which have been reported in general extrasensory perception are often repeated in supernormal photographic experiments. Amongst the most important of these is the 'decline effect' first noted as long ago as 1926 by G.H. Estabrooks, an American researcher, and since confirmed many times, which shows that in a long series of experiments the proportion of positive results will decline as the series of experiments proceeds, and the 'sheep-goat effect' which describes the findings also confirmed by many observers that the subject's attitude towards an experiment tends to affect the results, those with a negative attitude (goats) often have a lower rate of success than those with a positive attitude (sheep).

It is only in research with gifted children who are talented psychokinetic metal benders, after the style of Uri Geller, that the decline effect does not seem to occur. With the delicate and sensitive experiments which we conduct in experimental supernormal photography we must try to screen out any dampening effects and it is obviously sensible to work with sympathetic helpers and subjects as far as is possible.

Post mortem survival is not just a theoretical possibility, it is part of humanity's subliminal knowledge. We know that in many cases departed spirits not only exist as self-aware beings but that they also make their existence known to us and the knowledge of their existence is expressed in the almost universal practice of praying for the wellbeing of our departed ones and in the Hindu belief in the reincarnation of souls which pre-supposes the independent post mortem survival of our souls or spirits. Spiritualists have produced much evidence in favour of the hypothesis of life after death but, however convincing such evidence is, absolute proof still eludes them and will probably only be finally produced by photography, which is yet another reason for making photographic records of seances whenever possible.

In the USA John W. Edmonds, a Supreme Court Judge, began his enquiries into what we now call psychokinetic phenomena in January 1851 but it was not until April 1853 that he was ultimately convinced of the reality of the phenomena that he had witnessed. He said: 'I had recourse to every expedient I could think of to discover imposture and to guard against trickery . . . I have seen a mahogany table, with a central pillar and carrying a lighted lamp, rise at least a foot above the floor in spite of the efforts of those present to prevent it . . . I have seen a mahogany chair turn on its side and move backwards and forwards along the floor without being touched by anyone, in a room where at least a dozen persons were sitting, without any of them being touched by it. It often stopped a few inches from me, having been moved so quickly that had it not stopped, my leg would have been much bruised'.

The results achieved by Judge Edmonds and many other investigators were confirmed by the carefully conducted experimental investigations conducted by many eminent scientists of the day including Dr Robert Hare, Professor of Chemistry at Harvard, who became finally convinced although he had commenced his enquiries as the most sceptical of all.

Daniel Dunglas Home was probably the most powerful medium of his day, and this Victorian 'Uri Geller' demonstrated his abilities on many occasions before the leading figures in London. In 1868 he conducted demonstrations before Mr Varley, Chief engineer of the Atlantic Cable Company, before members of the London Dialectical Society, then under the presidency of Sir John Lubbock, and later before Sir William Crookes. Mr Varley reported: 'In my house, where Mr Home had never before been, 7 ft behind him there was a small table. Mr Home asked me to hold his hands, and placed his two legs over my left knee. After a few minutes the table began to move, and was pushed towards me by an invisible power, no person being near it, and while I was firmly holding Mr Home's hands and feet. A large couch capable of seating eight persons was pushed right across the room, and obliged us to move aside.' He adds, 'Deception was impossible'.

Members of the Dialectical Society held 50 seances with Home at each of which 30 people were present and they reported numerous examples of psychokinesis amongst the many varied types of phenomena that were produced. Sounds appeared to come from pieces of furniture, the floor and from the walls, often accompanied by vibrations perceptible to the touch, all produced without any muscular or mechanical cause. Movements of heavy bodies took place without any kind of mechanical action being involved, often without contact or connection with any person at all, and 13 persons deposed to having heard well-executed pieces of music from instruments not manipulated by any ascertainable agency. In one particular experiment which they declared decisive, 11 members of the society turned the back of their chairs to the table and knelt on them, feet behind and away from the table, hands resting on the chair-backs. The gas was alight above the table. Under these circumstances the table moved four times, and then, when the chairs had been placed a foot distant from the table, it again moved 13 times in different directions and in obedience to verbal demands.

Taken at a seance with Mrs Ada Deane, supervised by F.W. Warwick, on October 30 1823 this nonpsychic photograph shows the loose biplane top being lowered physically on to the table to be levitated to demonstrate that it is in fact a loose top.

This photograph shows that the hands are all on the loose circular biplane and that the table has levitated from the centre of the circle of wire mesh which prevents anyone touching or moving it physically.

In his book *Researches in the Phenomena of Spiritualism* Crookes gives a full account of the very exact experiments he conducted with Home and describes the instruments he devised for mechanically registering the movements produced in the form of a graph. He also tells of several other exciting experiences with Home. 'My own chair twisted round, my feet not touching the floor. Under the eyes of all present a chair moved slowly from a distant corner of the room. In another case an armchair came nearly up to where we were sitting and at my request moved back about 3 ft. On five different occasions, a heavy dining room table rose from a few inches to a foot and a half off the floor while I held the hand and feet of the medium.'

On one occasion an accordion which Home held by the finger tips of one hand in a cage made of wood and copper wire swayed about and played different airs. When Home let go of the instrument and placed his hand on that of a spectator the accordion floated around the cage and continued to play!

'One of the most amazing things I have seen,' Crookes says, 'was the levitation of a glass water bottle and tumbler. The room was well lit by two strong alcohol-soda flames, and Home's hands were far distant. The two objects remained suspended above the table, and by tapping against each other answered 'yes' to questions.

'They remained suspended above the table for about five minutes, moving in front of each person and answering questions. We verified that Home was entirely passive during the whole time and that no wires nor cords were employed. Home had not entered the room before the seance.'

People have questioned the genuineness of the phenomena produced by Home, but in point of fact no slightest proof of fraud has ever been put forward. Crookes says: 'To attribute these results to fraud is absurd. What I have reported took place in my own house, where nothing could be prepared in advance. A medium sitting in another part of the room with several persons observing him attentively, could not by any fraud cause an accordion held in my hand, keys downward, to play, or make it float about in the room playing all the time . . . He could not bring an instrument to move the window curtains, tie a knot in a handkerchief (and) put it into a distant corner of the room, cause the notes of a distant piano to sound, raise a water bottle and tumbler off a table, cause a coral necklace to stand up on one end, move a fan and fan the company, or set in motion a clock shut in a glass case firmly cemented to the wall.'

Russel Wallace quotes the experience of Robert Dale Owen, in which the medium was probably Home, as another outstanding and indisputable example of psychokinesis.

'In the dining room of a French gentleman, the Count d'Ourches living near Paris, I saw on October 1 1858 in full daylight, towards the end of lunch, a table laden with fruit and wine at which seven persons had been seated rise off the floor, all the guests standing round it without touching it.'

Eusapia Palladino, the Italian peasant girl who became one of the greatest physical mediums of her time, also produced outstanding examples of psychokinesis. At her seances she would fall into a trance and then, she claimed through the agency of her guide John King who was said to be the brother of Katie King and the father of Eusapia herself in a previous experience, was able to move objects without touching them and materialise the hands and sometimes the head and body of John King and also occasionally those of other phantoms. It was commonplace for Eusapia to put her hands 18 ins or so above a heavy table and, whilst her hands, feet, knees, waist,

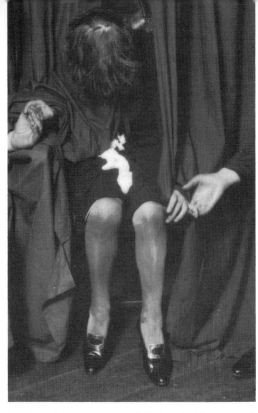

Left *Dated October 2 1928, this is one of a series of photographs taken by F.C.E. Dimmick showing ectoplasm exuding through the clothes of the medium Mrs Henderson.*

Right *Stereoscopic photograph of one of the ectoplasmic images produced by the medium Eva C (Martha Béraud).*

head and mouth were all being held, cause the table to rise up off its four legs without contact of any kind.

In 1892 Charles Richet, the Nobel prize winner who was a noted physiologist and parapsychologist, and some of the most outstanding European psychical researchers conducted a series of experiments in Milan with Eusapia Palladino. During the tests conducted by these Milan Commissions Palladino exhibited a remarkable series of phenomena which included materialisations, table levitations, and many other examples of psychokinesis. Describing Palladino's mediumship Richet wrote: 'Suffice it to say that doubt is no longer possible'.

Although it was shown that Palladino was not above helping out her talents physically upon occasion, many other seasoned researchers including W.W. Baggally, Hereward Carrington and Everard Fielding, three of the most eminent investigators from the Society for Psychical Research who went to Italy in 1908 to test her abilities, all certified that she produced the most incredible displays of psychokinesis under the strictest of investigations.

J. Ochorowicz, who co-operated with Richet in many of his research projects, was present at a series of experiments with Eusapio Palladino when Richet had a one metre square table weighing 44 lb especially made with pointed legs so that it would be difficult to raise with a foot. As soon as Eusapia touched this heavy table with her finger tips, it tilted, swaying about, and without the legs being touched at all, it rose up completely with all four feet off the ground. No ordinary physical explanation of this levitation was possible. There were no hooks or cords, the thing took place in half light and Ochorowicz and Richet were holding Eusapia's hands and head.

Ochorowicz made an intensive study of the psychokinetic ability of Stanislawa Tomczyk a young Polish girl who was able to draw small objects like a ball, a box of matches, a small handbell, or a needle through the air towards her and keep them up long enough for photographs to be taken even in a moderate light, which,

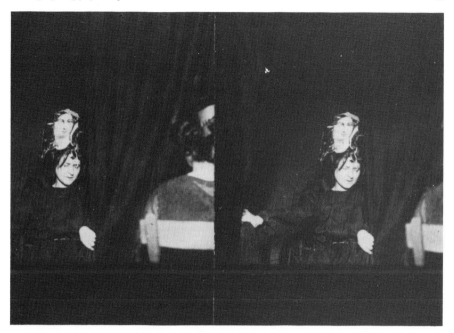

considering the slowness of the photographic materials then available, was no mean feat. Stanislawa turned up her sleeves to the elbow, washed her hands in soap and warm water, after which her hands remained always in full view and a commission of physicians, physiologists and engineers, who carefully verified these facts at Warsaw, certified to their entire authenticity. Ochorowicz saw Stanislawa producing even more powerful psychokinetic phenomena than this and suggested that the forces involved which he called 'rigid rays' seemed to proceed from Stanislawa's hands or fingernails and, describing one occasion when this happened, said: 'A chair behind me suddenly moved. It was a garden chair, light, painted red, and quite open in make. In full light it made little forward movements. *I interrogated it!* It raised itself on one side and gave one knock, then advanced a few centimetres. I placed my hand against the chair and felt a slight force pushing it.'

Many of the psychics who produced psychokinetic phenomena also produce other physical manifestations and materialisations. In a report of a series of experiments conducted with Linda Gayzera at his home in 1905 Professor Richet wrote: 'I held Linda's two hands, her head and her knees. A hand seemingly from behind me strikes me heavily. I think I can distinguish its fingers, and this is repeated a second time. I hold the left hand firmly, Imoda [Richet's friend E. Imoda was assisting him] holding the right which I frequently verified by touch. The objects were taken from the cupboard behind, a thimble was put on the first finger of my left hand, a sheath (etui) was put on my nose, and I felt fingers touch my nose and face.'

On April 19 1905, at home in Richet's library, a photograph was taken of an ecto-plasmic extrusion from Linda Gayzera. George de Foutenay is seated on the right and Mme Argentina on the left. 'The hand which appeared high above behind the curtain was released by a fluidic thread from the head of Linda. One could see the nails and all the falanges.'

'In the last experiment, the best of any,' Richet continues, 'no one was present

but myself, Mme Charles Richet and Mme F. I held Linda's hands *the whole time* (underlined in my notes), so that I can be absolutely certain that she did nothing with her hands. Mme F's chair was taken from her and removed to the middle of the room, then given back to her; I received a flower that I had placed on a shelf as high as the cupboard hardly to be reached by the hand, and higher than the head. I was touched by something from behind the curtain, though I could not affirm that it was a hand.'

Richet goes on to say: 'Telekinetic experiments succeed well with Linda and she is more easily controlled than Eusapia, for she scarcely moves at all, while Eusapia is in continual jerky movement. In the first experiments the ectoplasmic hand that I felt was cold and stiff; in the fourth experiment it was warm, articulated and supple.'

Eusapio Palladino exhibited all the variations between movements produced by a solid seeming materialised hand or rod of ectoplasm and movement produced at a distance without anything being visible at all, and the long series of experiments conducted by Mme Bisson and Baron von Schrenck-Notzing with Eva C and those of J.W. Crawford with Kathleen Goligher also showed this same great variation in the visibility and apparent solidity of the ectoplasmic materialisations which exerted the psychokinetic force that moved objects at a distance from the medium. This variation in intensity of the phenomena produced has led many investigators to theories that psychokinetic movements and poltergeist activity are the first steps in the materialisation of the physical solid-seeming bodies like those of the spirit 'Katie King' photographed by William Crookes during his researches with Florence Cook.

The objective reality of the materialisation phenomena has been affirmed by so many of the most reliable and eminent psychic experimenters and researchers that they are now established beyond doubt. This emanation of ectoplasmic substance and its shaping into organised forms has been witnessed and photographed on many occasions and the coinciding of the phenomena reported by so many witnesses forms a body of scientific material which must be accepted by even the most sceptical of enquirers. Such materialisation of an amorphous substance which first appears as a formless vaporous emanation slowly condenses into a solid seeming form that takes on the appearance of anything from that of ectoplasmic rods of force to the images of real people.

Sir Oliver Lodge noted in *Light*, May 14 1921: 'Concerning the kind of phenomena so well studied by Dr Crawford on which attention has been focused by the photographs taken by Baron von Schrenck-Notzing, Mme Bisson, Dr Geley, and the SPR Committee, I observed somewhat similar things under less favourable circumstances during my earlier sessions with Eusapia on Professor Richet's small island in the Mediterranean many years ago.

'A protuberance emanating from the medium's side (clothes being no obstacle) was sometimes seen by me, in dim light, as a whitish solid-looking but otherwise amorphous structure, and when the end reached one of those present he announced either that he was touched or that he was grasped by a hand.

'Hand-clutches on the arm or neck of one or other of those present were probably the most frequent form of manifestation with this particular medium at that time; indeed they were so frequent as to become commonplace.

Opposite *A spirit hand can be seen rapping on the underside of the table in this rare photograph of ectoplasm taken at Mrs Everett's circle by William Hope in February 1931.*

'Usually the protuberances were felt and not seen even when there was light enough to see them by. Sometimes they were seen and not felt presumably because they did not reach far enough to effect contact.

'On one especially distinct occasion, sitting outside the group, I silently watched a protuberance for about a minute stretching out again, till it succeeded in touching the back of Mr Myers who immediately exclaimed that he was touched, although he knew nothing about the tentative efforts to reach him nor of my silent observation of those attempts!'

Materialisations of a similar nature have been observed all over the world and, although the descriptions may vary in detail, they almost all agree on the main facts.

Mme Bisson, who began working with the medium Eva C in 1909 and took many photographs of her materialisations in collaboration with Baron von Schrenck-Notzing, noticed from their first sittings together that Eva's head and face became covered with a kind of whitish substance which transfigured her appearance. The subject observed by Mme Bisson and Dr Schrenck-Notzing and other researchers under the pseudonym of 'Eva C' was Martha Béraud, the daughter of a French officer stationed in Algiers. She had been engaged to General Noel's son but he had died in the Congo before the wedding could take place. The report made on Eva C by certain members of the Society for Psychical Research in January 1922—Messrs Dingwall, Baggalay, Fournier d'Albe, Woolley Fielding, Whately-Smith, Mrs Salter and Miss Newton—told of the materialisation of masses of a mobile substance, organised as hands, faces and drawings which emerged from her oesophagus or stomach and papers which seemed to be unfolded, put away and pass through a veil fastened over her face even though the medium's hands were tied and being held.

Mr Dingwall reported that, on one occasion, he also saw ectoplasm emerging from the medium as a miniature hand which moved and made signs to him before disappearing.

Martha Beraud's mediumship was also responsible for the materialisation of the phantom of Bien Boa who was claimed to have been an Indian Prince. Bien Boa appeared five or six times under vigorously controlled experimental conditions during a series of experiments carried out by Professor Richet in Algiers during which Martha and the phantom were both seen at the same time with Bien Boa walking and moving about.

Geley, who conducted research with Mme. Bisson and Eva C for two years, described two types of materialisations, solid and vaporous, that appeared both at seances at Mme Bisson's house and in his own laboratory.

'The solid substance is made up of an amorphous protoplasmic mass usually white occasionally grey, black, or even flesh colour. It emanates from the whole surface of the medium's body, but especially from the sides, the fingers, or the natural orifices.

'The gaseous substance resembles a more or less visible mist, sometimes faintly luminous, which usually seems to proceed from the medium's head. In this mist bright points of condensation appear, the light resembling that of a glow worm.

'Whether the substance is vaporous or solid it is as a rule very rapidly organised and then gives perfect or imperfect materialisations. Both are apt to give off light, the forms being sometimes luminous in whole or in part!'

To this precise description I must add that I have taken photographs of mediums which show just such gaseous or vaporous substances rising from the medium's

The entranced medium Eva C and an ectoplasmic hand coming through her dress.

head, although they were not visible to the naked eye at the time, and I also have photographs taken by other photographers which show similar examples of both experimental and spontaneous emanations of this kind which were not visible when the photographs were being taken. The solid and vaporous emanations are sometimes materialised simultaneously. At times the solid forms out of vaporous beginnings and at others the solid-seeming materialisations form first and gradually fade away into impalpable vapour. The materialisation of a whole body is the most spectacular effect, but more often one just sees a face or, perhaps, a hand growing out of a formless mass or appearing as if projected or superimposed on to the materialised ectoplasm, the medium, or the background.

All kinds of partial materialisations may appear with physical mediumship running the full range from complete or incomplete bodies and parts of bodies to floating veils, cottonwool-like clouds or wreaths of smoke and all kinds of organisms can be seen growing out of or superimposed upon them. Photographs have been taken under strict conditions of all these various phenomena and there is no reason why you cannot repeat them yourself. Many of these experiments can be carried out in good light and if you have to use flash the extremely short exposures given by modern flash guns and flash bulbs are usually well tolerated by mediums and, of course, infra-red flash is often not noticed at all. The important thing to do, once you have found a medium or group who can produce physical phenomena, is to adjust your photographic methods to suit them and not to insist on them sitting in conditions that suit you.

In *Experiments in Psychical Science* and his subsequent book *Psychic Structures at the Goligher Circle* W.J. Crawford gives many details of his experiments with

Kathleen Goligher, an amateur medium, and in his second book reproduced many of the photographs taken during their sittings which showed how Kathleen had produced table movements, levitations and materialisations of many kinds.

Kathleen Goligher was one of a poor Belfast family. Her three sisters and her young brother all showed some psychic abilities but Kathleen became a powerful physical medium. William Jackson Crawford DSc, a lecturer in mechanical engineering at Queens University, Belfast, investigated the Golighers and conducted a series of experiments with Kathleen between 1917 and 1920 during which, by causing knocking and rapping, levitating tables and extending psychic arms and rods both visible and invisible, she convinced him of the reality her psychokinetic talents.

In *The Psychic Structures at the Goligher Circle* Dr Crawford published a flashlight photograph, taken at an early stage of the investigation at the Goligher Circle, at which Kathleen Goligher was the principle medium and which shows just such a psychic extension. The circle had assembled with the object of obtaining flashlight photographs of the table being levitated, Dr Crawford having satisfied himself that this was achieved by some sort of psychic structure or force being extended from the medium so as to act as a cantilever with one end firmly fixed to the medium and the other end supporting the table or as a lever with some part of the psychic structure resting on the floor so as to provide a fulcrum, the mechanical reaction being the same in either case. The circle sat in its usual order with the medium at the top end of the room and the camera was placed near the bottom end facing the medium and was focused upon the table. The seance commenced with questions being answered by raps on the table and by the table itself levitating. This went on for about half an hour and culminated in the table being levitated and kept in the air for several minutes. After further discussions with the 'operators' who controlled the medium, Dr Crawford agreed to try the flashlight when the table was not being levitated, as he said, 'with the object, it seemed to me, of discovering what would happen to their psychic system of equilibrium when the powerful light should suddenly burst forth'. They decided to expose a plate during the flash, although they did not expect any result and were amazed at the picture produced when the plate was developed., Unfortunately the glass plate negative has been accidentally dropped and is badly cracked but the psychic structure which was invisible at the time can be clearly seen. It is obviously not a reflection and it is most unlikely that these markings could have been caused by chemical action during the development of the negative. The photograph was taken by flash powder, and not by magnesium ribbon, and the flash was placed on the camera about 9 ins behind the lens so the markings could not have been caused by the flash. The structure seems to be a beam of irregular shape supported at two ends by Kathleen Goligher and her young brother Samuel Goligher. It is visible almost all over its length but is densest at the top of the vertical column.

Dr Crawford suggested that, although this beam of light is a structure specially prepared to show on the photograph, it is basically similar to the invisible working structures that might get below a table to levitate it. He compared the whitish cloudlike appearance of the matter in this structure with photographs of materialisation phenomena obtained with many different mediums all over the world and came to the conclusion that this material closely resembles, if it is not identical with, the material used in all materialisation phenomena. The degree of solidity of these materialisation phenomena varies from the nebulous translucent smoke-like substance which I have photographed with Bertha Harris and several other mediums to the almost solid-looking whitish rod or bar shown here.

Crawford showed that it is this type of structure, sometimes more or less visible sometimes invisible, extending from the medium, which creates the psychokinetic movement of objects with which the medium does not come into direct physical contact. He wrote: 'It should be clearly noted that this matter is not the only component of a psychic structure. It is the stuff with which the structure is mixed or manipulated to enable the basic part of the structure to act on ordinary matter. There is another component behind it in all cases, a component which appears to be invisible, impalpable, and generally speaking, outside the range of physical things altogether!'

Professor John Hasted, of London University, with whom I have spent some time discussing this matter has suggested that the Geller-type metal bending and metal breaking phenomena may be caused by a force field or extension of some kind passing from the medium which seems to have similar characteristics to this 'invisible impalpable component' postulated by Crawford. Crawford and his colleagues, who sat with the Goligher circle for several years, agreed that these psychic rods which issue from the medium's body can be varied in diameter and length and can be detected by the sense of touch even though they are not physical.

On Friday December 5 1917 Arthur Hunt and two friends who were present examined the floor and table and tested the strength of an example of levitation by pressing down as hard as possible on the table which had been lifted up in the air. Towards the end of the seance Hunt lay on the floor alongside the table, placed his right hand between the two nearest table legs and almost immediately felt the impact of a nearly circular rod-like body about 2 ins in diameter on the palm of his hand which was held palm upwards about 5 ins from the floor. He noted that the room was clearly lit by a gas jet encased in panels of red glass and he could clearly see his hand and the space around and beyond the table legs but he could not see the psychic rod that he held in his hand. Dr Crawford describes the end of a large psychic rod as a soft, dense plasmic, half solid, half liquid mass which either pushes against or grips the table by a suction process. On many occasions he placed a tin or box containing modeller's clay or putty within the circle place and the medium's control, operators or guides would on request make marks on the clay with the invisible ends of these rods.

On one occasion a table was levitated in the usual way and then turned over in the air bit by bit with little jerks until it finally remained levitated in the air upside down. All the time Crawford was standing right up to the table in strong light with all the floor space and the medium quite visible. The experiments were in the main conducted in good red light (the light was from a gas jet covered with red paper) and Crawford was in almost every case able to verify that there was no physical contact between the medium and the tables and other objects that were moved. He found that, although the flashlight that he used to photograph the experiment greatly disturbed Kathleen Goligher, it seemed to have no ill effect on the materialisation which she produced and thus many of his flashlight photographs were taken with the medium being sheltered from the light by a black cape. During some of these experiments Crawford placed the medium on a weighing machine and observed the alterations in weight during the levitation. The results were similar and he found that the weight of the medium and her chair was increased by the weight of the table

An ectoplasmic rod can be clearly seen in this photograph of a seance with Kathleen Goligher photographed by Dr Crawford.

being levitated. Crawford said: 'Everything takes place as if there were a mechanical link (invisible?) between the medium and the table.

'The substance that produces the psychokinetic table movements is a kind of lever or rod which emerges from the body of the medium and is reabsorbed into it. It can bend, turn, and direct itself, but cannot act at a greater distance than about a yard and a half. It can change its texture, becoming hard enough to give strong blows, and can lay hold of objects. Its dimensions are variable. It can pass through garments and woven materials if they are close to the body, but cloths, paper, and woven materials, at a certain distance from the body prevent the action of the force. Its end can adhere to objects to be lifted as though sticking to them. The composition of the ectoplasm could not be determined, and although it certainly proceeds from the body of the medium, no pressure is felt and no reaction is perceived.'

The theory that psychokinesis is caused by ectoplasm is probably correct and although each medium uses a different method and approach the proof of the pheno-menon is irrefutable. At one test seance with Kathleen Goligher, on September 6 1920, five cameras were used in charge of Mr Pollock, a professional photographer of Belfast. Mr F. McC. Stephenson who arranged the seance stood next to the medium's chair throughout. The members of the circle were thoroughly searched before entering the room set apart by Dr Crawford in his house. Mrs Crawford and two lady doctors were present. The camera next to the medium's feet had a wide-angled lens. Flash exposures were taken and the red light which was on throughout the seance was extinguished for a moment just before the flash photos were taken, except in the last photos when the red light was on all the time. The medium (Kathleen Goligher), her family, Dr Crawford and the members of the circle all agreed that every precaution should be taken to prevent any suspicion of doubt or fraud being held about the physical phenomena which were produced.

At times Dr Crawford records: '. . . when the medium had seated herself on her chair, I tied her ankles together with fine strong whipcord; then I tied her ankles to the back bar under her chair . . . I always stood beside her, and her hands were lightly gripped by the sitters on either side of her during the whole seance. The strings and knots were always found intact at the end of the seance. Indeed, it usually took me five minutes or more to get her untied, and oftener than not the strings had to be cut.'

These experiments took place in Dr Crawford's home and his wife examined the medium and supervised her dressing in the clothes that they provided for the seances.

Dr Crawford also designed special electrical apparatus which prevented the medium creating any fraudulent effect by moving from her chair, which was screwed to the floor, and as a further precaution during some of the experiments a wooden frame was placed round the medium's legs so that fraudulent levitation of the table was impossible. The cross bar at the top prevented her feet being spread out and the whole apparatus was screwed to the floor right up against the front of her chair. The table levitated between 20 and 30 times during the seance when this wooden frame was used for the first time, the longest levitation was for about a minute and a half and about 6 ins high.

A medical friend of Dr Crawford's who stood by the medium taking her pulse and monitoring her physical condition used a red flash lamp, in addition to the red electric light shining overhead, whilst Crawford stood on the other side of the medium and supervised the levitations. A strong gas light enclosed in a glass lantern was placed close to the medium so that she could be thoroughly observed during the phenomena. It was noted that the medium's pulse rate, which was 72 just before the seance, rose to 120 and the palms of her hands got a little moist and the fingers a little cold during the actual levitation of the table but neither her respiration nor temperature seemed to be affected to any degree.

Dr Crawford took a photograph at every seance for more than a year and it was not until after inumerable attempts that the first small patches of psychic plasma were photographed.

During the following six months by continuously photographing the seaces he obtained many photographs of the unstressed plasma and, although photographs of partial levitations were taken, his untimely death brought the experiments to a close before the photographic results were complete and, for this reason, no photograph of a completely levitated table was obtained.

After Kathleen Goligher was married she carried on with her psychic research and her husband, Mr Donaldson, assisted in the experiments by taking infra-red photographs during her seances. On March 27 1933, at a seance conducted in darkness, the medium's arms and ankles were each separately controlled so that any active movement of them would have removed a plug and so disconnected one of four electric light bulbs which were in a box the lid of which was a screen which shut out all except the infra-red rays. There were five people present. Mr Donaldson and his wife, who was the medium, Mr Goligher her father, Mr Smyth an old friend of the family and Mr F.M. Stephenson. Mr Donaldson controlled the infra-red light whilst Stephenson, who was watching the four lamps, sat on one side of the medium and Smyth sat on the other. When the seance was over all the plugs were as at the beginning. The ectoplasmic-like materialisation on the carpet in front of the medium's feet can be clearly seen in the photographs which also demonstrate the position of the cameras.

Photographs of supernormal phenomena are often taken by researchers working with a psychic on their own, but many are the results of collective experiments which entail a conscious or subconscious psychic collaboration between the photographer, medium and a group of assisting experimenters. I have conducted photographic experiments with mediums and psychics whose supernormal talents have ranged from clairvoyance, healing and materialisations to psychokinesis and telepathy, and they have all agreed that the best results only come about where this psychic rapport exists. One reason for the difficulty in replicating the results in many investigations into the supernormal is because the enthusiasm and mental attitude of the people concerned is always of paramount importance and the production of these phenomena tails off in inverse proportion to the scepticism and lack of conviction of those engaged in the investigation. The enthusiasm and positive approach of the psychic who can produce tangible phenomena is often not reflected by those who attempt to replicate his results in a laboratory. As a direct result of this they have little, if any, success and after their results are published further experimenters show an even further decline in their success rate until finally no results are obtained at all.

Mrs Bertha Harris, perhaps the outstanding British medium of her day, was the clairvoyant consulted by King George V, Winston Churchill and General Charles de Gaulle during the Second World War. She had much success with psychic and supernormal photography. In experimental supernormal photography it is without a doubt the medium or sensitive who plays the most important part but it is imperative that this psychic co-operation comes about between medium and photographer and that the latter does not remain just a mechanical photograph taker.

For the mental phenomena a medium sitting alone will often suffice but physical manifestations almost invariably need the association of a number of sitters to induce and reinforce the externalisation of the phenomena. A favourable environment must be established and experiments should be held reguarly and patiently as it will take time for the sitters to meld together mentally and psychically so that their latent forces can be drawn out and used by the medium. With time and patience the faculties of the medium are reinforced and increased by this association until, as the dynamic and material emanations become stronger and stronger, the physical phenomena of materialisation and psychokinesis slowly begin to appear.

Sceptics have complained that mediums like to work in darkened conditions, but so do photographers in their darkrooms, so we should understand that light can have a harmful effect on our experiments. Light can add to the difficulties of a seance in two ways. It can disturb mediums and prevent them entering into the trance-like state which so many find necessary and it often has a direct harmful effect on the production of materialisation. Indeed it has been said that the scarcity of physical mediumship in modern times dates from the introduction of electric lighting and the subsequent great increase in the level of illumination that we have come to expect and to work in. Modern apparatus, however, copes quite well with low levels of lighting and the use of infra-red films and the range of the new extra-

In this infra-red photograph a materialisation can be seen beginning to grow through the clothes of medium Jack Webber (courtesy of Ray Branch).

fast films in conventional cameras can be extended by image-intensifiers, laser technology, thermography and low light intensity video cameras so that the happenings in darkened seance rooms are no longer shrouded in mystery.

The value of using red light, rather than white, during seances is due to the lower intensity of light that it provides rather than the longer wave lengths employed, although some mediums cannot work in the shorter actinic rays of light. The effect of light on a medium who has entered a trance-like condition depends more on its duration than on its intensity so that the shining of a torch on the medium to see what is going on in the darkened room will be much more disturbing than the firing of a flash gun or flash bulb for the fraction of a second required to take a photograph. Mediums are natural sensitives and should be protected from shocks of this kind as much as is possible.

Modern investigators have tended to overlook the experience of the past which suggests that there are several rules which help mediums to achieve positive results. In the East it has always been claimed that meditation and vegetarian regimes are of great assistance in obtaining the mental and physical conditioning necessary for the development of mediumship and recent parapsychological and psychic experiments seem to bear this out. They also show that the health and mental condition of the medium and all concerned with the experiments, as well as their expectations and confidence, all have a direct bearing on the results achieved. Time and time again talented psychics who have produced startling results in familiar surroundings have been balked when surrounded by laboratory apparatus, strange instrumentation and the hard, cold faces of sceptics. A medium is instinctively distrustful of sceptical observers. Whilst in a trance he or she is defenceless and completely in the hands of those around him and brash and over-clever observers who have turned on lights or flashed torches during the seances to see if anything untoward was happening have caused great mental and physical harm to mediums.

As a medium becomes accustomed to the routine of a circle or group of experimenters and learns to trust them, psychic manifestations of different kinds will begin to happen and, at this stage, the proceedings should be gradually tightened up until the sittings are all conducted under strictly controlled conditions. If it is possible the sittings should be held in the same airy, well lit and comfortably warm room. The room and contents should be thoroughly searched immediately before each sitting and kept locked between sittings. I would suggest that, if possible, the medium should strip and be thoroughly searched at the commencement of each sitting and then dressed in clothes provided by the circle. A one-piece garment with fastenings or elastic at the ankles, wrists and neck will be comfortable for the medium and provide adequate security for the experiments. Lace-up boots or shoes should be provided, rather than slip-on shoes or slippers, so that no one will be able to suggest that the medium's feet were slipped out of the shoes in the dark.

If these precautions seem to be extreme when a group of friends are experimenting please remember that, when you become proficient and are able to produce and photograph physical phenomena, sceptics will immediately try to denigrate your work and you must be able to show that the strictest protocol was enforced. Great patience is needed and, at first, session after session can go past with little or no positive result but the excitement when phenomena do begin to appear is well worth waiting for. Once this happens there should be no interruption or disturbance until the sitting is completed, so all arrangements of loading and placing of cameras should take place before the sitting commences. With the aid of a long cable release modern cameras with motorised or power winders will allow you to take exposure after exposure without moving from your place in the circle, and ciné cameras can be used in a similar fashion. With some cameras, such as the Canon AE1 (an automatic 35 mm single lens reflex camera), which at the time of writing is one of the top cameras in the middle price range, the electronic selftimer can be used together with the power winder and once it is set off the camera will take a series of automatic photographs at ten-second intervals until the entire film is exposed.

Sittings with a medium often take place in partial or complete darkness but it is well worth while taking photographs even under these seemingly impossible conditions as I have a number of photographs taken in just these circumstances which, when processed, showed successful supernormal images. I have used medium speed 100 ASA black and white film with some success, and in difficult lighting conditions I give longer exposure to emulate the slow emulsions, long exposures and long development times used by psychic photographers in the past although, as we have seen by using modern high speed films and pushing them in the processing, photographs can now be taken in low light situations that were once no-go areas of photography. One great difficulty which has been recorded by many investigators is the injurious action of light on almost any kind of ectoplasm or materialisations. Coloured light has been tried and many mediums like to sit in red light perhaps in the hope that, in some way analogous to its use in photography, it will be less harmful than white light but, if it is less harmful, it is probably only because the red light is usually weaker than the white. Dimmer switches can be used to control the intensity of the light, whilst Sir William Crookes held successful sittings by the light of the full moon. In Brazil sittings have been held by the light of fireflies and other luminous insects, and various filters and screens have been tried in continuing efforts to discover a non-harmful light source. It has been found that, providing the light level is very low when the sitting commences, once the medium has entered into the trance condition or altered state of consciousness the intensity of the light can be gradually increased without harmful effect.

Ectoplasmic materialisations take many different shapes and forms when they finally appear and often a considerable time will elapse before there appears a recognisable image or object. Experimental and spontaneously produced phenomena sometimes have a cloud- or smoke-like appearance and, at other times, they have the appearance of fine muslin or net floating in the air and the images seen and photographed are often flat, incomplete or irregular.

The *Daily Telegraph* for Monday September 18 1978 carried a report on page nine, by Geoffrey Fletcher, of his colleague Elizabeth's haunted house in Bath in which one of the bedrooms is peopled at dusk each day by phantoms from the 18th century which are, curiously enough, only seen in profile, and this is only one of many such reports in my files which tell of the sighting and photographing of flat two-dimensional phantoms. Many of the successful photographs of materialisations taken by Professor Richet, Dr von Schrenk-Notzing and Dr Hamilton show this sort of flat, almost two-dimensional, image although in others the images when complete do seem to be three-dimensional and show some depth.

These photographs show that materialisations were produced even though the most stringent and rigorous precautions were taken, on occasion even going to the extremes of stripping the medium and conducting internal rectal and vaginal examinations to ensure that nothing is concealed about their person which might be used to produce fraudulent phenomena of any kind. A photograph by itself, however convincing, does not prove the truth or reality of any phenomena, but when supported by exceptional experimental precautions such as these and by the testimony of expert observers of scientific renown, photographers of supernormal phenomena provide convincing evidence of the paranormal.

Some of the extra images that show up on unusual photographs can be classified as 'Eastman Effects', that is, as markings caused during the manufacturing or processing of the film, but these can be readily identified as the manufacturers of photographic materials all have both large laboratories staffed by professionals whose sole *raison d'être* is to prevent any defect in their manufacturing process, and consumer relations departments whose job is to identify and correct any faults that might show up later in the exposed film or prints. Between them these departments manage to identify and screen out almost every conceivable inadvertent defect which might be due to the photographic process itself or be inherent in impurities of the chemicals or in defective apparatus that may have been used. Very few of the photographs showing extra images or unusual anomalies pass the eagle eyes of these experts without some physical explanation for them being discovered, sometimes as simple and prosaic as a defective camera or light reflections from objects inside or just outside the field of view of the camera.

In spite of all these elaborate precautions, however, people using these carefully screened and tested films, processed in constantly monitored machines, keep taking photographs that show inexplicable extra images which range from bursts of energy, clouds of ectoplasm and rods of light to fully detailed and often identified faces and places. Because the people portrayed in supernormal photographs are often no longer living, Spiritualists have always claimed that these photographs are further proof of their belief in life after death and many do, indeed, seem to bear out this hypothesis. However, with the advent of thoughtographers like Ted Serios and the Veilleux family in the United States and Masuaki Kiyota in Japan, who have the ability to produce psychic photographs showing extra portraits of the living as well as of the dead, parapsychologists are tending to look for alternative explanations for many of the phenomena of supernormal photography.

A professional portrait photographer in Lincolnshire, named Binns, who was not a psychic person or in any way interested in Spiritualism or the supernormal, saw when he developed the photograph that he had taken of a farmer named Warren, a superimposed face which proved to be that of a cousin of Warren's, a Mr Ground of whose very existence Binns was unaware. This man Grounds was at that time still alive but dying in a hospital 15 miles away. The plate was taken from a fresh pack and Mr Ground had never been photographed since his childhood.

My wife and I have many friends who have told us about experiences of this kind and as a result of my lectures and radio and TV broadcasts large numbers of people have written to me and sent me supernormal photographs that they have taken personally and told me of their experiences with the supernormal. Some of them have purposely sought the experiences by going on ghost hunts and deliberately seeking out the phantoms but, in many cases, the reverse has happened and the phantom presence has sought out and come to them instead.

One of our friends, Mrs Lily Kashner, who had no previous experience of psychic or supernormal happenings of any kind, became convinced after the passing of her late husband, Sandy, that he was still about in their flat and she was aware of his physical presence for many months. At first she just felt a slight chill from time to time and an awareness of someone with her in the flat but this faint presence soon became more and more physical. On several occasions she felt someone next to her in bed at night so strongly that she felt impelled to switch on the light to make sure that she was alone and at other times she felt someone caressing her in the private way that only her husband had known. She heard footsteps in the flat and doors opening and shutting without reason and often, whilst in her favourite armchair, she heard and felt a distinct knocking on its back. This loud and clear rapping on the back of the armchair, as if someone was trying to gain her attention, continued from time to time over a period of several weeks and when it occurred she was always aware of her late husband standing behind her as he had so often done in life. She had searched thoroughly when these phenomena occurred but could find no ordinary cause or reason for them. The affair reached a climax one evening when she was sitting in the armchair alone in the flat watching her TV and the rapping and knocking on the back of the armchair became so loud and persistent that, without thinking, she called out 'Oh, do stop it Sandy!' She felt a sense almost of relief and withdrawal and the knocking stopped and at the time of writing this, several months later, still has not returned. Mrs Kashner told me that she is sure it really was her husband Sandy whose presence she had felt and that, when she had recognised him, he became released from his earthly ties and peacefully passed on to whatever or wherever we go when we leave this world.

Another of our friends, Mrs Hilda Alberg, presents a different picture. As her husband Frank well knows, Hilda has been sensitive to supernormal phenomena since she was a child and she has a fund of personal psychic experiences to draw upon. She was the youngest of ten children and her mother unfortunately became blind during her birth. This, together with the fact that her mother was also psychic, led to a closeness between them that was more than just a mother and daughter relationship and this closeness led to Hilda joining with her mother in many experiences that were denied to her brothers and sisters. Particularly outstanding to her are the many occasions after her father's death when her blind mother went to the door to meet and greet him at the time when he usually came home from work or when she sat talking to him and listening to his replies as though he were still alive. One incident which left a vivid image in Hilda's mind occurred when she and one of her sisters were washing up in the kitchen after dinner one evening. Her mother, who was sitting at the kitchen table behind them, started conversing with their late father once again and Hilda's sister happened to glance around and cried out, 'Good Lord, dad really is there!' Hilda turned around, too, and clearly and distinctly saw her late father sitting smiling and chatting to her mother both so engrossed with each other that they ignored the presence of the watching children. Although this is the only time that anyone else in her family has had such an experience Hilda has been involved in them on many occasions.

As so often happens with sensitives the psychic talents involved have waxed and waned over the years and for a time nothing of this nature occurred to her but, after her mother passed away, phenomena built up about her once again until, on many occasions whilst doing the housework in her home, she has looked up and seen her mother watching her. Once, whilst dusting the stairs in her house with her vacuum cleaner, Hilda saw her mother walking down them and she was so real and solid that Hilda was afraid that she might trip over the wires and called out to her, 'Mother be careful!'

Another time, whilst in the kitchen preparing dinner for her family one evening, Hilda heard her mother call her name and turning round saw her seated at the kitchen table. Walking over to the table, Hilda sat down facing her mother, and they spoke about the family, their past and future for a while until her mother got up and walked out of the room.

Mr and Mrs Alberg did not think of taking a photograph of any of these appearances, although both now agree that a photograph would be positive proof that the appearances were objective rather than subjective and they have promised to try to have a loaded camera handy about the house in future.

It has been argued that even the taking of a photograph showing an extra phantom image is, of itself, not proof that the phantom was physically present as it might be only a figment of imagination produced by the subconscious mind of the participant who had the further talent of impressing such images on to the photographic emulsion. Such theories would, however, only seem to complicate the problem and not to simplify it and, in any case, they imply the acceptance of both the existence of forces outside the bounds of our present day knowledge and the talents to control them and the very existence of such pictures would show how little we know of the subtle energies of man and their interaction with the physical world past, present and future.

The suggestion that these photographs are thoughtographs created by those people with the total recall that gives them a photographic memory and with the ability to externalise these images with sufficient force to impress them on to photographic film or paper also implies the acceptance of the modern theories of bio-energies and human force fields. Our bodies give off radiations or aura of several

distinct sorts. These include almost all the different wavelengths of the electro-magnetic spectrum, which are variously the result of electrical activity of the nerves, muscles and brain cells and the electron orbit changes which are constantly occurring in our bodies, as well as the actual chemical emissions that we give off as a result of our interchange with the atmosphere and the spectrum of sound given off by the movements, rotations and vibrations associated with the physical actions of our bodies as well as many other so far ill-defined and difficult-to-detect etheric and psychic emanations. We are only equipped to detect a few of these radiations naturally. We can sense that small section of electromagnetic spectrum that includes light and heat, we can smell and taste a small part of the vast range of chemical emissions and we can hear a limited section of the sonic wavelengths which are available. With the help of our instruments and machines we have learned to extend our senses and detect and make use of the long radio waves, X-rays and the ultra short gamma emissions. We have also learned to listen to the inaudible ultrasonic wave lengths of sound. We have learned to use the, so far unidentified, radiations involved in dowsing radiesthesia and radionics and a few of us can detect thoughts and move material things without coming into contact with them. However, in the main we are deaf and blind to most of the radiations and vibrations that surround us and which are too subtle or, perhaps, too great for us to perceive and which only break through our natural barriers and affect our senses at times of great physical stress.

Mrs Elsie M. Ball of Manchester, who wrote to me after hearing one of my radio broadcasts about psychic photography, has told me of her experiences which demonstrate the existence of just such force fields and energies as these. Her husband was in a nursing home and although he was not too well there was no immediate cause for anxiety until the morning of September 17 1976. That morning Mrs Ball was sitting on a settee, together with her nine-year-old grandson playing cards with him prior to his leaving for school at 9 am, when a picture of a Hay Wain that was hanging over the fireplace, and which her husband often used to stand in front of and admire, suddenly left the wall, sailed through the air and

In the next photograph, taken a few seconds later, the energy has built up to a burst of light. The photographs were taken with a Kodak Instamatic 25 using flash. The light was visible in the room but was not as pronounced as in the photographs (courtesy of Mrs Susan Simpson).

dropped face downward in front of their small table leaving Mrs Ball and her grandson petrified. She told me that, fortunately, there was no glass in the picture but when she examined it there was a clean cut in the string about 4 ins from the side fastener. Both fasteners were quite secure and there was apparently no reason why the picture should fall. If the string had weakened why did the picture not fall straight down? Did the picture fly away from the wall without any apparent reason as a warning of an impending tragedy, or was Mrs Ball's husband reaching out and trying to communicate with her? We will never know the answer to these questions but what we do know is that, on the evening of September 19, Mrs Ball and her son were called to the nursing home as her husband's condition suddenly deteriorated. They sat at his bedside for two hours and, although her husband had gone into a coma, Mrs Ball was able to hold his hand which was a great comfort. I must use her own words to describe what followed.

'At 7.20 pm after a last gasp for breath I saw what appeared to be a dull silver cord coming from the front of his head. It was twisted and before it left my husband's head it gave a little jerk as though it was completely freeing itself and then it went upwards until it disappeared.'

Mrs Ball asked me if she was given this wonderful privilege of seeing her husband's soul leaving his body because of their love and spiritual closeness or if it was because she was holding her husband's hand when he passed away thus saw this wonderful happening. Whatever the reason there is no doubt that she was indeed granted a rare privilege, and her description tallies vividly with that given by people who have experienced astral projection or other out-of-body experiences and who also describe a silver cord or cord of light which connects them to their body and which draws them back when they return to normal consciousness. Such silver cords or connections have been described and even illustrated by many astral travellers but they have never, to my knowledge, been photographed but, with the availability of the modern wide aperture lenses and ultra-fast films that make photography in dim light so easy today, there is no reason why such photographs should not now be taken.

Photographs taken of people at the point of their passing have on many occasions shown bursts of psychic energy and extra images that are associated with super-normal photography. Such bursts of energy and luminosities are seldom visible to the eye and if they are some form of physical energy they do not seem to be part of the ordinary visible spectrum but the existence of such luminosities of various degrees of visibility have long been known to parapsychologists.

John Beattie of Clifton, who was a skilled professional photographer, conducted a number of experiments with supernormal photography and was successful in producing a series of photographs which showed bursts of light, flaring luminosities and ectoplasmic images more than 100 years ago. His accounts of his experiments can be found in the *British Journal of Photography*, 1872 and 1873, the *Spiritualist*, July 15 1872, and the *Spiritual Magazine*, September 1872 and November 1873, and a further account less full than Beatties, by Dr Thomson, is given by 'MA (Oxon)' in *Human Nature*, September 1874.

In 1872 Beattie arranged to use the studio, glass, instruments and assistance of Mr Josty, a professional photographer, and was aided in his experiments by his friends Mr Butland, who was a good trance medium, Dr Thompson and Mr Tommy. The first day nine exposures produced nothing of interest. The second day, in the ninth exposure, an abnormal appearance developed itself which they could not account for. Up to this time Josty had laughed at the whole affair but this appearance, Beattie tells us, staggered him a little. On the third day an appearance presented itself which gradually changed and developed on successive plates. During one of the exposures, Josty, having uncapped the lens, suddenly went into a trance, from which he awoke much frightened. 'After that took place, for the rest of the evening he could not be induced even to touch the camera or slide, he was so superstitiously afraid.'

The next day no results were obtained; the next time 12 exposures were made with no results, and at length both Josty and Butland being entranced, Josty after uncapping the lens, moved to join the sitters during the exposure; on this occasion a white figure came out in front of him, just leaving his head exposed. Josty did not, he said, remember having placed himself among the sitters. After this it seems to have been arranged that Josty would sit with the circle, Dr Thomson uncapping the lens. Josty described during three exposures fogs which came out as described, and Butland said on one occasion that he saw a figure before him which duly appeared on the plate. At the next seance there was only one result out of 15 attempts. And at the next, strange flames are said to have appeared, in each case minutely described by both mediums as to number, position, and brightness during exposure. At the last seance three exposures succeeded out of 21. Mr Beattie says that he himself did 'all the photographic manipulating' and they 'closed every door from which there was the remotest suspicion of wrong getting entrance'.

In 1873 the experiments were repeated 'along with the same gentlemen and under the same conditions' and although the results in this second series seem to have been more striking, Beattie's description of them is less complete than the first. Again there were far more failures than successes. There were two mediums present, presumably Butland and Josty as before.' The medium next the background, we are told, became entranced and then by his influence he caused the other to pass into some strange, spiritual condition.'

The second medium (Josty) described during the exposure the appearances which were later found on the photographs, usually strange lights of varying shapes, developing through a series of three or four exposures. On one occasion he said, 'it rose up and over another person's arms, coming from his own boot'. On another occasion one medium said he saw a black figure and the other a light one. Both appeared on the plate but rather faintly, the light one indefinite in form. The results of the two series seem to have been 32 successful photographs.

Dr Gustave Gelley reported seeing light materialise during seances on many occasions describing them variously as slightly phosphorescent vapour, self-luminous hands and faces, a trail of white and slightly luminous vapour whose form was constantly changing, brighter points appearing in it. At other times the lights seemed isolated, often taking the form of nearly circular discs from the size of a ten pence piece to that of a crown.

At other experiments he recorded that two lights, like small half moons, met and formed a single indistinct mass then vanished, lights came, rapidly increasing in brightness, and the lights are as described on previous occasions, nebulae, phosphorescent vapour, very brightly luminous points and large luminous spheres, etc.

Jean Guzich, an outstanding Polish medium of the 1920s, is on record as having produced many impressive lighting and psychokinetic phenomena. During some 50 seances in Warsaw with the Polish Society for Psychic Research and 80 sittings at the Metapsychic Institute in Paris, the psychokinesis and materialisations that appeared were often accompanied by luminosities of various kinds. The lights usually formed near and mostly behind him and the focus of emanation was nearly always at a short distance behind or at his side sometimes appearing like glow worms in size and brilliance whilst, on one occasion, Dr Gelley reported seeing, 'a luminous pillar as high as a man, at the top rounded like a ball, about the size of a head. This vanished and was succeeded by coupled lights two and two behind the medium'.

'Two of these came close to my face,' he continued, 'and I saw clearly the face of a young man with an aquiline nose, the upper and lower parts of the face are veiled. It disappeared after two or three seconds.'

At other times observers present saw many bright lights and outlines of luminous faces, a whitish pillar, a luminous hand, and many flying lights, luminous rays and spheres and zig-zag flashes, but I can trace no photographs of these manifestations. Similarly, during experiments with Eusapia Palladino, lights like white or phosphorescent clouds were often seen moving about her head but these, too, do not seem to have been photographed.

Lights and bursts of energy that are visible but cannot be photographed seem to occur as often as those which, although not visible to the naked eye, do appear on photographs. Several witnesses have told me that Mrs Bolder of Milford on Sea near Lymington, Hampshire, has the ability to produce luminosities and flashes of visible light about her in a darkened room but no one has yet been able to photograph them. At the urging of Mrs S.M. Simpson of Lymington my elder son Jeffrey and I visited Mrs Bolder during one tour of the south coast of England in November 1976. I broadcast from many of the radio and TV stations and we visited many psychics and healers en route and, during the first week in November, we spent several hours with Mrs Bolder in her home. She worked herself up to a very tense state during our interview but no lights appeared whilst we were there and although we spent some of the time in a darkened room with the curtains drawn and an hour or so in a small completely blacked out darkroom, no lights or luminosities appeared on any of the

The circle of observers were holding each other's hands and the arms and legs of the medium Jack Webber were tied to his chair whilst this table floated unsupported in the air (courtesy of Ray Branch).

many photographs that we took with three cameras using black and white infra-red film, both slow and fast black and white and colour 35 mm film, and Polaroid instant print films.

Mrs Bolder's house is situated on the corner of a street leading to the sea front and the front itself with a wonderful view out to sea. It was a glorious autumn day when we had arrived, the sun had been blazing down and people had been sun-bathing on the beach but, as we were standing in the hallway taking our leave, without any warning a tremendous 'tropical' storm blew up with surprising suddenness and although our car was parked in the drive immediately outside the front door, my son and I were soaked through as we dashed out through the pouring rain, almost continuous flashes of lightning and roars of thunder to the car. As we drove out of her little drive with the downpour drumming on the roof of the car we passed through a curtain of rain into blazing sunshine again and my son called out in surprise and brought the car to a sudden halt shocked by what we saw. We were on the sea front in brilliant sunshine, people were still swimming and sunbathing on the beach, everywhere that we looked the sky was blue and clear and the sun was shining brightly except for directly above Mrs Bolder's house where there hung suspended a large black and dark grey swirling cloud with lightning playing under it and thick solid-seeming rain pouring down from it soaking the house and the small piece of ground that it was standing in. I turned to take a photograph of this amazing scene only to recall that we had used up all of the five 35 mm films and two packs of Polaroid film that we had brought with us and were left with three empty cameras, and we finally drove away with the mocking echo of the thunder ringing in our ears without a single photograph of this astounding sight.

Needless to say, since then I have always made a practice of carrying a spare loaded camera in the car whenever we go on such trips but, of course, nothing like that has happened to us again.

Matthew Manning is one of many accomplished psychics who have reported lights and luminous effects sometimes preceeding and sometimes during the exercise of their various and varied talents but, because there was no loaded camera at hand, these too have often gone unrecorded. The association between psychokinesis and visual paranormal phenomena is clearly shown in the work that has been done with Matthew Manning.

Manning's ability to bend small metal objects and deflect compass needles paranormally has been demonstrated and photographed on many occasions and, needless to say, the experimenters have satisfied themselves that the keys, knives and forks were not bent by trickery and that Matthew was not wearing a ring, wristwatch or any other metal object when he moved the compass needles, usually by passing his hand about 6 ins above them.

There are fads and fashions in paranormal and psychic phenomena and it is these effects on metal that are fashionable at the moment. Psychokinetics is one of the most fascinating fields of parapsychology and, unlike the allied phenomena of clairvoyance, precognition and telepathy, is one that lends itself to the production of photographic evidence of the paranormal. The ability of a talented few to move or otherwise affect physical objects by a paranormal power of the mind, sometimes controlled by forceful concentration and at other times overflowing in outbursts of polergeist activity, is one that is possessed in a greater or lesser degree by many and is one that can very often be improved by practice.

That the human mind can influence matter directly by non-physical means has been demonstrated not only by psychics like Matthew Manning and Uri Geller but has also been clearly shown by the scientific experiments in psychokinesis, or PK, that were started by Dr J.B. Rhine at Duke University in the 1930s. He showed in a carefully controlled and recorded series of experiments that the fall of dice could be influenced by the thrower to a degree beyond the realm of chance. A die has six sides so there is one chance in six that any side will be face up when the die comes to rest and statistical evidence shows clearly that some people can score more than chance expectation.

Dr Rhine's PK evidence has been studied and confirmed and his experiments replicated by many other investigators using as subjects people as diverse as divinity students and gamblers, trying to influence things as different as the fall of the ball on a spinning roulette wheel and the rate of bursts of energy recorded by a Geiger counter registering the radioactivity of a uranium salt.

This paranormal effect of mind on matter is shown in thoughtography, the non-physical production of images on the light sensitive emulsion of photographic film or paper, demonstrated in the past by experimenters such as Professor Fukurai of Tokyo University, psychic photographers like William Hope and more recently by many modern thoughtographers. The close connection between supernormal photography and the other paranormal powers demonstrated by people with psychic abilities has also been shown in experiments conducted by those researchers all over the world who have been able to work with supernormally talented people.

In *The New Soviet Psychic Discoveries*, Souvenir Press Ltd 1979, Henry Gris and

William Dick reported that Dr Genady Sergeyev, a Russian doctor of engineering and a mathematician who lectured in the Medical Centre of Leningrad University and at several Leningrad hospitals and institutes, had conducted and witnessed many scientific experiments with the famed psychic Nina Kulagina which showed that her strange mental powers could be recorded on photographic film. Kulagina's supernormal psychic abilities were first reported in the early 1960s. Her fingerprint vision was the first remarkable talent that was noticed. She can perceive colours by just touching them with her fingertips, and scientists investigating this unusual ability soon found not only that this was a genuine talent but that Kulagina also had the power to heal open wounds, cuts and abrasions by merely laying her hands on the affected place and that she was occasionally able to transmit and receive the thoughts of people around her.

It was, however, her talent for psychokinesis that made Kulagina into such an outstanding success with parapsychologists. By putting all extraneous thoughts out of her mind and concentrating exclusively and wholly on the target object she could move small objects such as matches, cigarettes and table tennis balls and even cause them to be suspended in thin air. Dr Sergeyev found that it was possible to record this powerful psychokinetic energy radiated by Nina Kulagina. During a series of experiments in Leningrad he put fresh photographic film into a black lightproof envelope and found that by concentrating and looking, as it were, right through the envelope she could 'expose' the film inside. Gris and Dick saw prints of the photographs produced during these experiments which clearly showed irregularly-sized white dots scattered all over the photographs. Interestingly similar dotted images have also been produced by the Japanese boy psychic Masuaki Kiyota in Tokyo and by a young British paranormal metal bender during a series of experiments conducted by Professor John Hasted in London.

In their book *Psychic Discoveries Behind the Iron Curtain*, Sheila Astrander and Lynn Schroeder give an account of an interview with Dr Zdenek Rejdak, Scientific Secretary to the Czechoslovak Coordination Committee for Research in Telepathy, Telegnosis and Psychokinesis. Dr Rejdak told them that the committee had not only filmed psychic experiments and the production of psychic phenomena generally but were also producing three new films on parapsychology covering dowsing, telepathy and supernormal photography.

More than 47 films of Nina Kulagina's psychokinetic talent in action have in fact been made and Russian cinemas have shown a film entitled *The Secrets of our Brains*, produced by Kiev Films, which shows Nina and other Soviet psychics in action. In these films she can be seen mentally causing small objects to jump and roll about, matchboxes to move and compass needles to spin all without touching them or influencing them physically in any way.

In some of them the tests are conducted inside insulated Faraday cages and Nina is seen to be completely monitored by electronic devices in attempts to pin-point the bio-physical influences involved in her talents. She is connected by electrodes to electroencephalographs to measure her brain waves, electrocardiographs to measure her heartbeats and even more esoteric electronic instruments designed to measure and record the fluctuations in her bio-energetic and other biological fields.

Researchers have found that both Nina Kulagina and Alla Vinagradova, another psychic, create large increases in the electromagnetic fields surrounding their bodies when they move objects paranormally and that their heartbeat races to as much as

240 beats to the minute—three or four times the normal rate—whilst the magnetic fields around them pulsate at the same frequency. This, together with the electro-encephalograph recordings of their brain activity which show enormous levels of activity in the visual areas of the brain when straining to move objects without physically touching them, suggests that they visualise a future state when the object has changed its position and in some way create the conditions which make this new visualised position come about.

Similar impressing of an internal visual image on to the external world may be one possible way of creating thoughtographs and the action of externalising the internal image may itself be recorded on photographic film as has been shown in experiments where a roll of film covered by a black lightproof sleeve and fixed around the heads of these two and other sensitives has shown inexplicable and unexpected markings when developed.

The Russian film *Seven Steps Beyond the Horizon*, produced in 1969 by the Kiev Film Studio, showed amongst other interesting fields of research some of the work of Dr Vladimir L. Raikov, who not only regresses subjects through previous lives and incarnations whilst under hypnosis, but who has also been able to keep them aware of these past lives when they are awakened from the trance so that they retain the knowledge and skills that they had in their past lives and can use them in the present.

A Czechoslovakian film shows a series of devices and instruments which are powered by human psychoenergy from a distance. Some of these machines are moved by and measure the psychokinetic forces involved whilst others are psycho-tronic accumulators and generators which seem akin to Reich's Orgone generator.

Russian parapsychologists have found that solar activity at the time of birth has an affect on psychic ability, those born when there is considerable sunspot activity being usually better projectors of telepathic messages and so might well be better projectors of images for thoughtography. The phases of the moon also seem to have some influence and supernormal abilities of all kinds seem to be more powerful when the moon is full. There are solar cycles which peak at 7-, 11-, 35- and 80-year intervals and it would be interesting to check these periods of great outflowing of solar energy with planetary cycles and the biorythms of man to see how they interact with each other and how the disturbances that they create affect our human force fields.

Scientists have divided the physical energies that bind the Universe into four main groups, the electro magnetic, the strong binding energy, the weak energy found in the interactions of the elementary particles of matter, and gravity which, although it seems to affect us most, is in fact the weakest one of all. As our knowledge progresses through the scale from the stronger to the weaker energies we have found that there is no barrier between them and that we are gradually getting nearer to the concept of the non-physical energies which are capable of being modulated by biological systems and so can be used to produce the phenomena displayed by the talented sensitives and physical mediums which we have labelled as apports, levitation, materialisation and psychokinesis.

Most mediums say they are little more than an instrument for amplifying or inter-preting these energies but Spiritualists go further and claim that these energies are used by the spirit world to communicate with the living and they have, indeed, produced much evidence to support this claim, including large numbers of psychic photographs which they say have been produced paranormally by the use of just such non-physical energies. I will not repeat here the enormous mass of evidential proof of post mortem survival that has been accumulated in more than a hundred years of serious psychical research but the archives and libraries of the Society for Psychical Research and the many old established Spiritualist organisations will amply repay a visit and will rapidly dispel any doubts as to the ability and honesty of the investigators, the thoroughness of their research or the correctness of their theories which show conclusively that there are energies or forces which are so fine, impalpable or weak that we are as yet unable to identify them or record them with ordinary laboratory instruments but which can nevertheless be modulated by the human psyche or biomechanism so as to reveal tangible traces of themselves on supernormal photographs. That this psychoenergy can be controlled and used to produce psychoenergetic phenomena that illustrate every aspect of the supernormal has been shown repeatedly in laboratories all over the world and the realities of these energies have been shown in many different ways.

Healers have shown that such an energy flow or force field exists between their hands and the bodies of their patients and Dr Robert N. Miller, an industrial scientist conducting research in chemical engineering in Atlanta, Georgia, has even shown that the cloud chambers used by nuclear physicists to detect high energy particles and the energies released when they collide will also detect the energies of some healers.

The July 1974 issue of *Science of the Mind* reported the experiments that he conducted with the internationally acclaimed healer Olga Worrall. Using an Atomic Laboratories model 71850 5 ins high and 7 ins in diameter cylindrical glass cloud chamber, with a glass plate covering the top and its metal bottom covered by a layer of methyl alcohol and standing on a block of dry ice so that as the alcohol evaporated the chamber filled with a misty vapour, the healer was asked to hold her hands away from the glass on opposite sides of the chamber and to visualise herself treating a patient in an effort to transmit the healing energies between her hands. The vapour in the cloud chamber not only showed a strong wave pattern developing between Olga Worrall's hands but, when she moved their position 90 degrees, the wave patterns also shifted so that they remained parallel to her hands.

Dr Miller found that, unlike many other experiments of this nature, this one was repeatable. Olga Worrall has since shown that she can produce this wave effect in the cloud chamber from her home in Baltimore which is 600 miles from the laboratory and the famed psychic Ingo Sann and two other subjects have also obtained similar results.

Healers, people with telepathic talent or the ability to move physical objects by psychokinesis, metal benders, psychic photographers and Spiritualist mediums are the obvious candidates for this kind of experimentation but such research is more aptly left to those with well equipped laboratories, as are the many experiments now being conducted using physiological instrumentation such as the electrocardiograph, electroencephalograph, galvanic skin recorder and plethysmograph in efforts to detect and trace the elusive psychoenergies.

For the majority of us it will be enough to prove that these energies both in their unmodulated form and after they have been modulated by a living organism can be captured and recorded simply and clearly by photography.

Poltergeists and similar supernormal psychokinetic phenomena which seem to be in a direct confrontation with our normal physical laws have two possible sources. They may be either the result of the direct mental effort of a frustrated personality bursting into violent unrestrained physical activity, or else they are the expression of an external intelligence associating and interacting with the unconscious agent at the centre of the poltergeist or psychokinetic activity. If this activity comes from some hitherto unsuspected aspect of the human psyche then we must find out how to release it from the bounds of the subconscious and bring it out into our conscious minds, and should it really prove to be caused by some external agency or intelligence then we must learn how to bring this under our conscious control.

People have learned how to control the autonomous nervous system of their bodies so that they can control their blood pressure, breathing and heartbeats well enough to survive being buried alive for long periods without harm and, with the aids of modern biofeedback methods, there is no reason why we should not be able to extend this control to that part of the human psyche that is capable of bursting out of the confines of our everyday four-dimensional existence so that we will all be able to make use of these supernormal talents that can give us mental control of the physical universe.

One difficulty that is found in the investigation of supernormal photography is caused because we are possibly lumping together several different types of phenomena which all register on the sensitive photographic emulsion. Spiritualists' psychic photographs, parapsychologists' thoughtographs and the photographs of healing forces and ectoplasm taken by psychic healers may well originate in different ways and may even be brought about by different types of energy. Very little energy is needed to affect the photographic emulsion and, although the energy that is radiated from the human body and brain is minute it may be strong enough in especially gifted people. It may well be, however, that this human bio-energy is not the operative factor itself but is primarily used to modulate or influence energy that already exists in the environment.

Modern research into the many different kinds of supernormal phenomena is gradually being accepted by the scientific establishment because of the more and more sophisticated technologies that are being used to document and record the elusive forces entailed. Electronic equipment, however, is not the entire answer and leading scientists all over the world are gradually realising the importance of photography in this field.

The answer to all the queries and misunderstandings about psychic photography is once again to do it yourself. Thanks to Messrs Kodak, and the legion of other camera manufacturers, almost everyone today has a camera of one sort or another and for the purpose of psychic photography the simpler the camera the better. There is no need for the elaborate modern single lens reflex with built in automatic light meters and exposure systems and although, of course, these can be used too, the simple Instamatic will serve as well as any other camera for early experiments but, if you do not have one, even an old box camera and a roll film will serve as well. Without being too sophisticated it is sufficient just to cover the lens of the camera with a lens cap held on by elastic bands or adhesive tape or even with a piece of black card held firmly so as to exclude all light and then, holding the camera in front of you with the lens pointing towards your face, concentrate on a simple image such as one of the designs on a pack of Zenner ESP cards or perhaps a tree, or a fish, and try to project the mental image on to the surface of the film. This experiment can even be done in a darkened room which may help you to concentrate and, if there is no light coming in to the room at all, you can try this with the lens uncovered or you might try to replicate the Ted Serios experiments by holding a gismo just in front of the lens but not touching it. The results are very simple to evaluate as, if you have taken the necessary precautions to exclude all extraneous light, any image on the film must have been produced paranormally. A series of these experiments can be conducted with very little expense using black and white film. Naturally the film need only be developed to ascertain the results and it will only be necessary to have prints or enlargements made from those negatives which have images on them. The use of Polaroid or similar cameras giving instant photographs is a much more expensive way of going about things but the immediate results that they produce have the great advantage of keeping up interest in a series of tests and the production of one positive result is always a great incentive to carry on and produce more.

Only a few years ago evidence of supernormal photography was still being brushed aside and ignored but the accumulating evidence of such photographs is making the most hardened sceptics think again and many highly respected researchers are showing a renewed interest in the entire subject. Discussing the meaning and nature of the paranormal in his presidential address to the Society for Psychical Research, in October 1975, Dr John Beloff said, 'The first difficulty that one encounters in this connection is to know which phenomena one can take as authentic'. He went on to say: 'The peculiar fascination of psychic photography, psychic healing and materialisation phenomena is that here one seems to be confronted with mind in the act of imposing form and order on amorphous material. Consider what is implied by a genuine psychic photograph. The molecules of silver chloride, or whatever makes up the surface of the sensitive film, must organise themselves in such a way as to correspond with an image in the subject's mind . . . .'

Here again, of course, the resultant photograph can be seen and handled by all who are interested and, once again, we can produce physical proof of the supernormal which in this material world is the only thing that will substantiate our claims and provide a basis for the new theories that will perhaps unlock the secrets of another dimension for mankind. This book contains a tiny fraction of the overwhelming evidence of supernormal photography and anyone studying it with an open mind can hardly escape the conviction that the phenomena follow definite, if so far undefined, laws. These laws hold daring implications for the future that may be more important than the discovery of atomic energy or laser technology. Nuclear fission is something that happens in the external world but the phenomena recorded in supernormal photographs come from inside us. This is an interior revolution in mankind of such great potential that no one can foresee its full outcome.

The most widely differing types of cameras, films and techniques have been used to record supernormal photographs and, although many successful photographers have worked out their own systems, some of the most important supernormal photographs have been taken almost by accident. The only successful way to approach the subject is to pick up a loaded camera and take photographs.

Chapter 3

Modern supernormal photography

We all have the innate ability to produce psychic phenomena of one kind or another and supernormal photographs have been taken by people in all walks of life. Amateur photographers, Press photographers, professional portrait photographers, psychic healers, Spiritualist mediums and people with no interest in either photography or psychic matters have all taken psychic or supernormal photographs at one time or another, sometimes indeed finding them to be such an embarrassment or so damaging to their profession that they have been discarded or destroyed before anyone else has seen them.

The wedding photographs of Mrs Joyce Simmons of Blackheath, daughter of Major C.H. Mowbray, are an example of this. When she was married in Blackheath church in April 1937 many of the photographs that were taken of the family arriving at the church had unexplained extras on them. It may have been the photographer who was the medium as the photographs with the extra images each show a different group of the guests. In this case Major Mowbray, who was a Spiritualist, saved the photographs.

The early psychic photographs of Mrs Bertha Harris, whose lifetime of experience with psychic matters makes her a living link with the early psychic photographers, were also taken as wedding photographs. When she was a girl her father, Arthur Hindle Hughes, a low paid civil servant, augmented his income with photography and Bertha acted as his assistant. To her father's annoyance his photographs were often spoiled and a day's work lost because of the extra images and what he called 'those damned ghosts' that appeared in them. After a while he realised that these extra images only appeared when Bertha was assisting him and she was promptly banned from his photographic sessions.

As Bertha grew up her psychic talents developed. She became a Spiritualist and had been working as a medium for several years when Lady Conan Doyle introduced her to William Hope who was producing psychic photographs with Mrs Buxton as his medium. Mrs Buxton became ill and was in hospital for several months in 1930 and during this time Hope made many visits to Bertha's home in Chester where they experimented and together produced many successful psychic photographs.

Mrs Harris' talent for psychic photography has waxed and waned, as all the psychic powers seem to do from time to time, but she has been instrumental in producing psychic photographs when working with several other photographers all of whom were men. She told me that in her experience one of the factors necessary was the presence of a man and a woman working together and that even then there

Left *There was no one at the organ when this photograph was taken by Robert Harris with his wife Bertha Harris acting as the medium.*

Right *St Clara Cathedral, Stockholm, Sweden, built in 1577. 'There were no living persons in the pews when I took this picture.' A.Z. Nelson Peterborough, NH, USA, April 25 1981.*

could be no control over the appearance of extra images on the photograph. When she was with Spiritualists she said that they usually sang hymns, prayed or meditated together but this seemed to have no real relevance to the production of the extras which seemingly came of their own volition. A London detective, Mr Tomlinson who was a Roman Catholic, a friend called Freddie who prefers to remain anonymous and her husband Robert Harris, who was a trance medium, were amongst those who were successful in taking psychic photographs with her after William Hope died in 1933.

Although there was no one at the organ in their home at Chester in 1939 when her husband Robert took the photograph illustrated the psychic image of a man can be clearly seen. There are many recorded instances of phantom organ players. When his life story was featured in a BBC2 television programme early in 1976 comedian Michael Bentine told of the organ in the church at Borley in East Anglia which he had investigated with his father, Adam Bentine. This phantom organ player is also mentioned in *The Ghosts of Borley* by Peter Tabori and Peter Underwood published by David and Charles, 1973, where it is reported that the Reverend A.C. Henning, Rector of Borley with Liston, heard the organ of Borley church playing at about 3.15 pm on an afternoon in October 1947 and, knowing that there was no service at that time, rushed into the church but found to his amazement that it was completely empty and quiet. He had been just outside the south door of the church with Mrs Norah Walrond (better known as the novelist Norah Burke) who had also heard the organ music and helped him to search the church. Although this is the only time that Mr Henning had heard this phantom organ himself it has been reported and investigated on many other occasions.

Inexplicable music of this kind has been reported from many other churches including spectacular incidents at the parish church of Cressing, near Braintree in Essex, in 1950 when music was repeatedly heard whilst the church was locked and empty. However, the photograph by Robert Harris is the only psychic photograph showing a spectral organist that I have ever seen.

Mrs Harris has had a remarkable career as a medium but no psychic extras appeared on her photographs for many years until recently, as her gift seems to be returning, and in the last year or so two other photographers and I have obtained photographs of her with inexplicable anomalies and extras on them on several separate occasions. A new phenomenon is also appearing and psychic extras are now showing on portraits of her that were ordinary photographs when they were first taken many years ago. This is the first time that this has happened to any of Mrs Harris' photographs but I have had a similar experience myself when extras recently appeared on a series of photographs that were perfectly normal when first taken three years ago. There are flash-light photographs of my miniature bonsai trees which I took at night on my terrace with the night sky as a background. There is nothing unusual about the negatives and when the prints were first made they were perfectly normal but when my younger son Philip took them out to show them to a friend a little while ago he discovered that inexplicable extra images have appeared on all of them. Whether these supernormal extras have appeared as a result of my working with Mrs Harris or because of my own latent talents in this direction I do not know, but there have been psychic influences in my life and these together with one confirmed case of telepathy and my small but positive talent as a water dowser have led to my having a very open mind on these matters. The very expression 'an open mind', which is part of our language, shows that we are subconsciously aware of the fact that some people's minds are negative and closed to thoughts and impressions and outside influences whilst others are open and responsive to more than just the gross physical world.

The appearance of supernormal extras long after prints are processed is not something that is new or confined to the photographs of a small number of people but, like all supernormal photography, is universal and spread throughout the world. When I was in Miami, in the spring of 1976, I had a most interesting discussion about supernormal happenings in the United States with Jackie Head, Pastor of the Spiritual Research Society Church in Orlando, Florida, and as a direct result of this

The interior of Eastry Church, Kent, photographed by a bank manager in September 1956. There were only three people in the church at the time—all behind the camera! (courtesy of Andrew Green).

she gave my name and address to LeRoy Christopherson when he showed her a 16 × 20-inch colour print of a woodland scene on which the image of a person praying had suddenly appeared almost five years after the photograph was taken and three months after that enlarged print was made. LeRoy Christopherson is convinced that this particular image came about because of a deep and very significant religious experience that happened to his wife Alice in 1971. He began his story of the events that led up to the appearance of this remarkable supernormal photograph by saying, 'Believe me, having a 16 × 20 colour print (pictorial scene), on which an image of a person in prayer suddenly appeared, is indeed a mind-boggling experience'.

'It all began on Sunday, October 24 1971. At least that's when I made the original exposure on 2¼ CPS neg film. I had flown up to the Iowa Minnesota, area to attend Dad's polled Hereford sale the following Monday. I took my camera because I wanted to visit the farm where my wife and I had spent our first six years together (1954-1960). I wanted to photograph some fall scenes and show them to friends back in Orlando.

'However, nothing was ever really done with these scenes until January of 1976. We decided to hold a 'one-man' art show at the Winter Park Mall, Winter Park, Florida, and needed a number of large prints (16 × 20 and larger), to offer for sale. The scene in question was among those selected. In fact, we made six prints from this particular neg, because we knew it would be a popular sale item.

'In April '76, we had only two of the original six left. There were two events coming up which we wanted to take part in. First, an art show in Pine Hills (second week in April). Second, the Florida Professional Photographers Spring Conference in Fort Lauderdale, Florida, on April 24-26.

'One print was entered in the Art Show. It was sold. Then on April 20, I took the remaining print to be critiqued at the regular meeting of the Central Florida Photographers Association, to determine if it was worthy of State competition the following weekend. The print was selected along with three others to compete in Intersection Competition against five other State Affiliate Sections.

'However, because of an infraction of a rule, this print was never judged in Fort Lauderdale at the Spring Conference. Following the Conference, I brought the print home, which had been in the print case since April 20. Setting the print case (containing the print) in the office I pretty much forgot about it. Then on May 18, needing the print case, I removed the print. What I saw nearly made me drop it. Staring down at the print, I saw a perfect image of a person in prayer. The image appears to be superimposed over the original scene.

'The print is 16 × 20 in size; has a high gloss finish; is colour—printed on RC paper and is dry-mounted. The Minnesota scene shows a small stream leading to a small clump of trees.

'The image is approximately 18 ins tall and 4-5 ins wide. It does not extend or bleed off the print. Also, the image is visible only when the light is striking the print at an angle. Viewing the print head-on, one can only see the beautiful Minnesota scene.'

I have a new colour print from the original negative of this scene and it is a normal photograph of a woodland scene with no sign of the supernormal extra on it but the colour print made in January 1976 and the black and white copy of it reproduced here clearly show the supernormal image of a person with his hands held up in a position of benediction or prayer.

Another interesting example of this delayed phenomenon was when Mr W.S. Bobby, the manager of the Palace Cinema, Market Place, Devizes, who lived in a flat over the Griddle Grill cafe next door to the cinema, complained of hearing an invisible presence softly climbing up the 12 carpeted stairs and apparently standing outside his bedroom door every night at midnight. He appealed to a local Spiritualist medium, Ivor H. Sercombe, for help and Ivor, accompanied by Dennis Kingman (a reporter) and Ronald Lewis (a Press photographer) who were then with the *Wiltshire News* waited with him at the flat on August 25 1962. They heard the footsteps climbing the steps and halting outside the door but although Ivor saw the figure of a bearded man wearing an old fashioned jacket tightly buttoned up to the neck and described him to the others, they saw nothing at all. Ivor sat alone outside the flat the next night and spoke to the figure who was a member of W.S. Bobby's family who had nothing to do with the building and did not know that he had departed this life. Ivor explained that he had passed on and asked him to stop calling as he was upsetting people and the man did not appear again.

Although he could not see the figure, Ronald Lewis had taken a series of photographs by available light on the previous night when they were all present. He told me, and the others confirmed that, although the negatives looked blank at first, after a few days the faint images of the man that Ivor had described became clearly visible on every frame and showed on several series of prints that were made on different grades of paper. Unfortunately the images were not contrasty enough for newspaper reproduction and the photographs are no longer available. The very nature of psychic photography lends itself to this type of result and I have seen many photographs showing psychic extras which regrettably cannot be reproduced in print.

There are many cases on record of photographs recording phenomena that were not visible at the time that the photograph was taken. Photographs that I have taken myself during experiments with Mrs Bertha Harris have often been of this nature. On the very first occasion that we met and spent a few hours together on March 1 1976 my tape recorder, which had been in perfectly good order and which I had tested before leaving my home, would not work when I arrived at her home. After I had been there for a while my canvas holdall which had been sitting squarely and safely on a chair decided to crash to the floor and it was because of this that we obtained the photographs with extras on them. We were talking generally about psychic phenomena when I began taking a series of photographs of Mrs Harris with a hand-held Contax IIa 35 mm camera using Kodacolour II negative film with automatic flash and, after exposing some 20 of the 36 frames, I carefully put the camera down on to the sideboard behind me and placed the flashgun safely in a canvas holdall that was sitting squarely on a chair and resting up against a corner made by the wall and the sideboard. I then picked up a model 230 Polaroid camera loaded with a 3,000 ASA black and white film pack which I exposed by available light.

Whilst I was taking these Polaroid pictures the holdall containing my flashgun seemed to leap up off the chair and crash to the floor, damaging the foot of the flashgun that attaches it to the camera and, because of this, I used the available light (one central 100-Watt bulb in a darkish shade) for the rest of the colour film giving an exposure of $\frac{1}{10}$ second at f1.5. The extra images appeared on these longer exposures building up from photograph to photograph from what at first looked like a wreath of smoke until, on the last one, nearly a third of the photograph was obscured by a mist or fog although the negatives both before and after those with

Below left *The supernormal image of a person praying suddenly appeared three months after this print was made in January 1976 (courtesy of LeRoy Christopherson).*

Below right *Taken at the presentation of a Union Flag to Joan of Arc's church at Domrémy, France, by Lady Palmer. The only people in the church when the photograph was taken were Lady Palmer and her friends, Mr and Mrs W.E. Foster, who were behind the camera. The two extra figures that appeared in the photographs were priests wearing archaic vestments (courtesy Miss V.S. Staff).*

Right *Ted Serios produced thoughto-graphs on the film in a Polaroid camera (courtesy of Jule Eisenbud MD).*

extras appearing on them were perfectly ordinary portraits of Mrs Harris. As is often the case with paranormal photography none of these extras was visible in the room when I took the photographs.

Another outstanding example of this photographing of the invisible is shown in a picture that was taken in the church of St Mary the Virgin, Woodford, Northants, in 1964 by Gordon Carroll, who was then 16 years old. Gordon, and his friend David Hasdell, who was with him at the time, enjoyed cycling about the country-side visiting and photographing historic old castles and churches. Woodford Church was mentioned in the Domesday Book and is worthy of interest so, on their visit, the young men took several photographs of the interior of the church and of the stained glass windows. When the slide in question was returned from processing there was nothing unusual about it and Gordon filed it with his growing collection of church interiors without seeing anything out of the ordinary and it was not until nearly two years later, whilst he was sorting out some slides for a Christmas show in 1965, that he noticed the ghostly figure kneeling before the altar. Gordon and his friend always asked permission of the parish priest and made sure that the church was empty before they took any pictures so as not to disturb anyone who might be saying their prayers. On this occasion they were both certain that the church was empty and that there was no one at the altar when Gordon took this photograph because they went up to where the figure is apparently kneeling and took another photograph from there of the other end of the church.

Father Charles W. Crawford of St Gregory's Church, Northampton, Gordon's parish priest, and Reverend L. de Casabianca, Rector of Woodford, whom I have questioned about this, both give the young men excellent references and agree that as devout Roman Catholics they would not play tricks about anything of this nature. Canon John Pearce-Higgins, as a member of the Church's Fellowship of

Psychical and Physical Research investigating the matter at the time, assured me personally that there was no question of fraud involved. Also, an expert at Agfa, the manufacturer of the film Gordon was using, agreed, 'There has been no trick photography used in taking this film, there has been no double exposure and there is no flaw in the actual film or fault in development'.

Completely blank film, sometimes clear as if no light at all has reached the film during the exposures and sometimes completely fogged as if the entire film had been bathed in bright light whilst still in the camera, but in both cases with no trace of any image, sometimes occurs in supernormal photography. On Tuesday March 16 1876 I spent several hours with Mrs Harris and used several different films and cameras in an attempt to capture the elusive extras which sometimes appear on her pictures. However, I produced, with one exception, only some very nice portraits of her. The exciting exception was a Kodak high-speed infra-red 35 mm film that I exposed in a blacked out room using a No 87 Kodak Wratten infra-red filter on my electronic flashgun and it was exciting because, aside from the fogging where light or heat had entered through the slit in the magazine, the entire film was blank. The film was fresh from Kodak and the fogging at the end, together with the existence of the photographic edge markings, show that there was nothing wrong with either film or the commercial developing process. The film had definitely passed through the camera as I had carefully checked that the rewind knob was turning each time that the film was advanced, both when I loaded the camera and twice during the session, and I noted the tension when I came to the end. A double exposure prevention device in this camera ensures that there is no possibility of two exposures being made on the same frame so that, in the highly unlikely event of the shutter having jammed by accident for just this one film, I should not have been able to use the camera at all. The only explanation for this film having passed through the camera and remaining unaffected by light is that the presence of Mrs Harris in some way either prevented the light from reaching it or prevented the light from influencing it. The flashgun was working, giving off a faint red glow when it was fired, and the camera was in perfect working order as I had used it the previous day producing a perfect set of negatives, and after collecting this blank film from the processors I immediately exposed another infra-red film in exactly the same way using my daughter as the subject in a similarly blacked out room but this time finishing up with all 20 frames perfectly exposed.

Similar results have been produced by other photographers working with Mrs Harris and other photographic mediums and Dr Jule Eisenbud records many instances in his book *The World of Ted Serios* when Polaroid pictures, which should have normally shown Ted Serios' face, came out perfectly black as though the light had been prevented from entering through the open lens. On one occasion, whilst in a television studio in front of a dozen close observers, Ted produced six of these all-black Polaroid prints out of about 50 tries and there was no sign of light on any of them, although several thousand Watts of studio lighting were streaming into the open camera lens each time the shutter was triggered.

The spectral monk who glides through the ruins of Bolton Abbey in Yorkshire

Opposite *The kneeling monk was not visible when Gordon Carroll took this photograph of the empty interior of the Church of St. Mary the Virgin, Woodford, Northamptonshire, in 1964* (courtesy of the Northamptonshire Evening Telegraph).

'I do believe it to be an angel, not the spirit of the deceased, who was an ordained Christian minister of the Foursquare International Gospel Church. At the time I took the picture, I asked all persons near the casket to step aside. There was no figure in my focus when I took the picture. Myself, none of the other four ministers, nor other persons present saw any figure. It only appeared on the photo as it developed. Also, there was no one at the services dressed in white.' This Polaroid SX70 *photograph and the quoted explanation are reproduced by kind permission of The Reverend Randall Grill.*

also defies the photographer. This abbey was closed and left derelict in 1539 as a result of the dissolution of the monastries ordered by King Henry VIII and an Anglican church has since been built in the shadows of the old ruins. There was at one time an Augustine Priory in the grounds and the ghost wears the robes which were customary before the modern hassocks came into use, complete with the white overlay which was the forerunner of the modern surplice. Reverend Griffiths, pastor of Bolton Abbey, and his wife who have often seen the figure and regard him as a friend, have noted that his appearances are usually accompanied or preceded by a pleasant smell of incense. I have not been able to get a photograph of the monk and the Reverend told me that, although many attempts have been made to photograph this priestly apparition, the photographs have always come out completely blank.

Far more people than is generally realised have this talent for producing supernormal photographs. In the course of some recent correspondence about the history of photography with C.S. Cowper-Essex, a one-time honorary officer of the Stereoscopic Society, I mentioned my research into supernormal photography and to my surprise he said he had a psychic photograph that he had taken himself. He was in no way psychic and was not interested in Spiritualism or supernormal phenomena in any way but told me that he had been taken to a seance, the one and only that he had ever attended, by a friend. 'I took the camera along on the spur of the moment,' he said, 'and asked the medium if I could take a photograph and what exposure to give. The reply was, "Just point the camera towards me and take a snapshot". This I did—not, of course, expecting any result. The result showed a streak of light coming from high up to the left of the medium and pointing towards her, and the faint outline of a face above where the medium was sitting. The camera was a Rollieflex, I used black and white Agfa film giving an exposure of 1/50 second at f4.5. The seance room was pitch dark, it was a dark evening and the curtains were drawn. There was no light leak in the camera and all previous and following photographs on the film were OK.' In response to further questioning he stated: 'There was no trace of image on the blank spaces surrounding the frame. I am positive there was no fogging or damage to the film during development, nor was there any mention of photography before the seance commenced—I am convinced the image was imprinted on the film in a supernormal way.'

There have, of course, been many more famous photographic mediums than can be mentioned here. Photography itself brought about a great change in the intensity of human consciousness and in our relationship with the outside world. The great value of supernormal photography is that it gives observable results of investigations into phenomena that were formerly outside the domain of physical laws. It is one of the few remaining fields in which an intelligent amateur can still make a significant contribution to science and, in fact, is probably the only field in which there are no scientific specialists with whom to compete. In the past many leading scientists were interested in psychic photography but, although modern physics shows that the distinction between the physical and non-physical properties of both man and matter are not as distinct as were once thought, and indeed in the search for elementary particles such distinction loses its meaning, scientists today seem to be unwilling to become involved with experiments of this nature.

Supernormal photography is a new science and the research and development of any new science depends firstly on the accumulation of data. When sufficient data has been gathered, the amount necessary depending on the subject and the level of its acceptance by the general public and the scientific establishment, this swelling mass of evidence itself induces the intuitive leap forward or the mathematical equation that unlocks the mystery. The very nature of supernormal photography makes such investigations both simple and straightforward and each of us by seeing if we can personally produce supernormal photographs can help to strengthen the mass of evidence that I have outlined here and so encourage others to join us in the search for the secrets of the supernormal.

Chapter 4

The Chelmsford photographs

One of the most amazing series of supernormal photographs that I have ever investigated was taken over a period of years at meetings of several different groups of people who were mostly scientific and engineering employees of the Marconi Wireless Telegraph Co Ltd, as it was then called, and whose success was mainly due to the photographic mediumship of one of their number who went on to become a deep trance medium and a most successful healer.

The medium who has given me details of these groups and allowed me to reproduce many of his photographs wishes to remain completely anonymous so that he will be able to carry on his investigations undisturbed, because he is convinced that any use of his talents for personal gain or notoriety would lead to them disappearing entirely. I can vouch for his personal integrity but, in order to make this account as factual and accurate as is possible, I have traced as many of the members of these Chelmsford groups as I could and almost all of them have been good enough to allow me to reproduce the photographs that they took at the meetings and to include their evidence here.

This medium's first introduction to Spiritualism came when he had gone as a complete sceptic to a meeting arranged by a new Spiritualist group at a school hall in Chelmsford in October 1960. He had left a warm car and entered the hall feeling comfortably relaxed but as the meeting progressed he noticed that the atmosphere was getting colder. He attended several seances experiencing only this occasional drop in temperature and seeing nothing out of the ordinary in the hall, although several of those present saw or became aware of several spirit guides or entities in one dark corner of the room whilst the meeting was in progress.

Several other members of the group also spoke of feeling chilled during the meetings and a thermometer showed a drop of several degrees each time this happened, so he took a camera loaded with an infra-red plate with him to the next meeting, fixed it to a beam in the ceiling of the hall and pointed it towards the corner in which the manifestations had been said to take place. Being an engineer he had no difficulty in fixing up a mechanism that tripped the shutter when there was a drop in the temperature and, by this means, a photograph was taken during the meeting. When it was developed, to his great surprise, it showed an Indian chief and several other spirit guides who had been described by the medium but had not been visible at the time. After his remarkable photograph appeared it became the practice for one or other of the members of the group to bring a camera along to the meetings and take photographs and usually at least one or two of the negatives had supernormal extras on them. Many different types of films and plates were experimented with. Black and white and coloured photographs, colour slides and Polaroid pictures were produced and supernormal images were also produced directly on glass photographic plates and printing paper without the use of a camera.

Several of those present showed traces of psychic talents. By experimenting and leaving the hall one at a time it was shown that my friend had become an outstanding trance medium and that the extra images that were appearing on their photographs were due to his mediumship. In order to develop his talents and extend his power of healing, he and his wife, who is also a medium with pronounced psychic gifts, organised a group of friends who met in their home, and many supernormal photographs have been taken there, although photography is a by-product rather than the main purpose of their meetings.

Carole Mayes, who has now blossomed out as a photographic medium in her own right, was a child of 12 at the time and suffering badly with diabetes. Her mother, Gwen James, who is also a medium, brought her along to my friend's meetings and her diabetes responded well to the psychic healing that she was given there. Carole was encouraged to bring her old Kodak box camera with her and to take photographs during the meetings and extra supernormal images appeared on several of the negatives. Some of these were not recognised but others were the faces of deceased friends and relatives of those present and Carole's own dead sister appears on two of them. One of the medium's spirit guides gave Carole great help with her spirit photography. He said that he was Dr Loyd A. Jones and had been a photographer in the United States before he had passed away. She was encouraged to investigate this claim and when she saw an advertisement for the Eastman Kodak Co of New York in a magazine she wrote and asked them if they had any knowledge of Dr Jones. Carole and all the group were astounded when the Eastman Kodak Co replied giving details of his life and confirming that he had indeed worked in their New York Laboratories for many years before he passed away in 1956. This is a good

The sitter, Dr John Winning, is completely obliterated by the spirit lady and the cloud of ectoplasmic lights seen in this photograph taken with a quarter-plate camera at the medium's home at 10.10 pm on January 18 1964 and developed immediately.

This paranormal photograph of the clock tower at St Albans was taken indoors in a small room in a house in Chelmsford in 1961, yet the facia and front of Halford's shop at the bottom right shows the property as it was in the late 1930s.

The facia and shop front of Halford's St Albans branch as it was in 1953 (courtesy of Halfords Ltd).

example of the veridical evidence that can be produced at these meetings. Verifyable testimony of this kind has been recorded and tested by Spiritualists for more than a century and is the basis for their belief in post mortem survival. It is strongly reinforced by supernormal photography which provides physical evidence of the unseen world around us.

Early in 1961 Marconi employees formed several other groups of this kind. Some of those who joined the groups were interested in spiritual and psychic matters generally but others just went along more or less out of idle curiosity. John Self of Halesworth, Suffolk, who was at that time a development engineer with Marconi, became a member of one of the earliest of these Chelmsford groups. John, who is now a maintenance engineer with the Central Electricity Generating Board, was introduced to psychic matters by Albert Lamb a fellow Marconi employee in whose Chelmsford home this group met. The meetings usually took place at about 7.30 pm. The curtains in the small room were not drawn but light was switched on as necessary so that there was just the normal lighting in the room. Those present sat around in a circle and the medium almost immediately fell into a trance. Soon various characters manifested themselves and in turn spoke through the medium. The same characters manifested week after week and were easily recognisable by their distinct accents and mannerisms. Some of the conversations were recorded. They were usually very faint to begin with but gradually grew in volume until finally the manifestations were talking loudly and clearly mostly in English but sometimes in a weird mixture of foreign languages.

My friend the healer was invited to attend one of these meetings at Albert Lamb's home and, as he was by then also well known as a photographic medium, John Self took his Weltaflex twin lens reflex camera loaded with Kodak Verichrome Panchromatic black and white film with him to the meeting. Following the instructions that were given by the medium's spirit guide John pointed the camera at several places around the room and took photographs by the light of the single 60-Watt bulb suspended from the ceiling, giving exposures of 1/25 second at f11. This is the setting for normal photographs in bright sunlight and in the dimly lit room it should have produced very thin transparent negatives with little or no image on them. John used three rolls of film giving 36 exposures in all and developed the film himself in front of everyone using a black changing bag to transfer the film into a daylight developing tank.

Those present could not believe their eyes when the film was removed from the developing tank and the first photographs were seen, for the dense negatives with the distinctly bright and unusual images on them could not have been produced normally in those circumstances and at no time were any of the supernormal lights or images that can be seen in many of the photographs visible in the room. Nine of the negatives from the first film had recognisable pictures of people, animals and scenery. Two showed only the bubbles, smudges or sparks of light that were also visible on some of the first nine negatives, and one picture was completely blank as should, of course, have normally been the case with all of them.

Five of the negatives in the second roll of film showed recognisable pictures, two had only the bubbles and smudges of sparkling lights and five were completely blank. The third film was completely blank from beginning to end. The blank negatives were completely transparent with no trace of image on them at all, in marked contrast to those that did have images which were exceedingly dense as if they had been exposed to a very brilliant light.

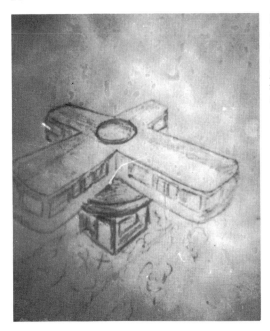

Left *This photograph of a drawing of a futuristic house built on a swivel so that it can be turned to catch the sun was one of a series taken by just pointing the camera to the centre of the room and giving an exposure of $\frac{1}{25}$ second at f11 by available light.*

Right *This photograph is apparently the house that is sketched in the previous photograph. Taken by pointing the camera towards the centre of the room and giving an exposure of $\frac{1}{15}$ second at f11 by available light during a seance conducted by a healer.*

Although they had appeared in such a remarkable manner none of the images on these photographs was recognised or had any significance to any of those present, and it was not until 1974 when John Self submitted the negatives and a report on the entire affair to the Borderline Science Investigation Group in East Anglia, who published the report in the spring 1975 issue of their quarterly magazine *Lantern*, that one of them was identified. This photograph shows a clock tower and, following up a clue given by a member of the group who noticed the name Halfords Ltd on the facia of a shop just behind the tower, John wrote to Halfords Ltd who kindly checked their records and, in November 1974, replied confirming that the tower shown in the photograph is indeed the clock tower in St Albans. They enclosed their own photograph of the shop, taken in 1953, for comparison and add to the mystery by pointing out that the shop front is different from that shown on John's supernormal photograph which they said shows the property as it was in the late 1930s, although there is no doubt that the properties are the same.

The sparkling blobs and streaks of light which can be seen in many of these super-normal photographs that were taken through my friend's mediumship are a distinctive feature and act almost as a signature since they appear regardless of who takes the photographs. Such lights have been seen in connection with psychic happenings in many places. Mrs Mabel Smith, the wife of the Reverend Guy Eric Smith, Rector of Borley 1928-30, often mentioned the little lights or sparks which appeared at the seance held in the Blue Room of the Rectory by Harry Price on June 12 1929 and Mr Williams, one of the occupants of the Rectory cottage at Borley in August 1953, reported seeing whirling circles of light similar to those visible in this series of photographs in his bedroom at night.

In the *Proceedings of the first Canadian Conference on Psychokinesis*, published by the New Horizons Research Foundation in June 1974, Mathew Manning also reported luminous lights which occurred during a violent period of poltergeist

activity in his youth. It happened on at least two occasions at night in his dormitory. One was a patch of light on the wall about the size of a dinner plate which grew to about 6 ft across as he watched and then slowly disappeared. On the second occasion a similar light appeared in the same room. These lights were first seen by a prefect of the school and were also witnessed by the school Matron. The second light grew until it reached from the floor to the ceiling although there was no light being projected on to the wall from anywhere. However, none of these lights was photographed and, as we have seen, those on the Chelmsford groups' photographs were not visible in the room when the photographs were taken.

Other members of the Chelmsford groups, using different cameras and films at different times, all produced similar results which are not explicable in ordinary photographic terms, and similar supernormal photographs have been produced on sealed glass plates and printing paper without the use of the camera at all. One of the most spectacular and exciting results obtained on glass plates exposed in this way was an X-ray photograph. A member of the group arrived in one of their meetings complaining of a bad pain in the back and, whilst still in a trance, the medium picked up one of a pile of photographic plates that another member of the group had brought along to experiment with and held it against the top of the painful spine. After a few moments it was developed and an X-ray photograph of the spine and upper part of the body appeared on it.

In another experiment, suggested by the medium's guide, black and white photographic paper in a light-proof wrapping was placed face downwards on a table and a vase of flowers was put on for a few minutes. Then, following the guide's instructions, the paper was washed in a developing tray containing a solution of glycerine in water and this, contrary to all expectation, produced a brightly coloured photograph looking like a primitive or childish poster colouring on the black and white printing paper, although there is no known way in which the

Psychic photograph of an airman who lost his life at Standstead Airport. Taken at Stanstead Hall in the first week of August 1965 with a healer as the medium. Exposure $\frac{1}{25}$ second at f11 in a darkened room.

unlikely combination of black and white printing paper and a solution of glycerine in water could have produced a colour print.

These groups met almost every week for several years, although not all the members were present at each meeting. Many of the members of the groups showed signs of psychic talent but most of the supernormal photographs appeared on the occasion when my friend the healer was the medium. When photographs were taken the negatives were usually developed at the end of each session in front of those present, a changing bag was used to transfer the films from the camera to a developing tank and the glass plates and printing paper were developed in open dishes by the light of a safety lamp with everyone present looking on.

During this same period another group was holding meetings at the home of Mr and Mrs Walter Eden in Chigwell. This group, which has met fairly regularly for many years, was made up of people who were deeply interested in psychic matters. Mr Eden is a medium and at one time the group included six other mediums but supernormal photographs were only produced at the few meetings which my friend attended and at which he was the trance medium. At one meeting, early in 1969, when my friend was the medium, Mrs Eden asked if she could use her folding camera which she loaded with a freshly purchased film.

The medium went into a deep trance and his control told Mrs Eden where to point the camera. Photographs were taken where the medium directed and the control was asked if some sort of identification could be put on to the photographs as some were taken by just pointing the camera around the room whilst others were taken with the camera pointing at certain of the people present. When they were finished Mrs Eden removed the film from the camera and it was developed immediately. Exposed for 1/25 second at f11 in a dimly lit room the negatives should have been thin and almost featureless but instead they were very heavy and many of them showed spots of light arranged in circles where people had been sitting and had arrows or lines of light pointing to different people in each of the pictures. Mr Eden and others of those who were at this meeting, and who I questioned separately about this, agreed that at no time did the medium come near to the camera or film until after the negatives had been developed and examined and that none of the extra images had been visible in the room when the photographs were taken.

My friend has been the medium and given healing at several other circles in the area and photographs taken whilst he was present at these meetings have also showed supernormal extra images. Those of one small group in particular were most unusual. They showed details and gave information of a technical nature which was highly prized by those present. He has also travelled extensively and photographs which have been taken of him at meetings all over the country have also shown unusual extras. During his visit to The Glasgow Association of Spiritualists in 1974 no pictures of any consequence were produced, but Dr John Winning of Glasgow was present on other occasions witnessing the purchase of the film, loading of the camera, taking of the pictures and developing of the negatives when remarkable results were obtained.

A number of the friends that he and his wife have made over the years have also developed this kind of talent and they have discovered other photographic mediums who have also become good friends. His wife worked in the same Ministry of Agriculture office and was friendly with Eleanor DeRoe for several years without either of them being aware of the other's deep interest in psychic matters until, one day, a chance remark revealed their joint belief in the spiritual world. At that time Eleanor DeRoe was attending the meetings of a philosophical group in Shenfield but, when she discovered their mutual interests, she joined my healer's group and was present when many supernormal photographs were taken there.

When the healer and his wife moved from Chelmsford their group split up and Eleanor DeRoe and her friend Florence Booker started their own group. They had five or six members attending their meetings and they were profoundly moved when they discovered that they, too, could produce supernormal photographs. Although the extra images appeared only intermittently they showed on some of their holiday photographs as well as on photographs taken at their meetings, one or two photographs with supernormal extras on them appearing unexpectedly in the middle of a roll of otherwise normal pictures.

Eleanor uses an old Kodak 44b 127 roll film camera and, as so often seems to be the case, extras appear on many different types of films. Those which I have examined include black and white negatives and prints, colour slides and coloured transprints made from them.

Chapter 5

Thoughtography

One of the most exciting discoveries yet made in the investigation of supernormal photographs is that some people have the ability to produce thoughtographs, that is photographs made directly on the photographic film or paper solely by their thoughts or mental powers and these thoughtographs, combining as they do both mental and physical phenomena, illustrate yet another of the varied ways in which we can interact with our environment.

Thoughtographs are often made without using a camera at all, the medium just concentrating his thoughts on to the sensitised surface of the film plate or printing paper being used in the experiment by, for example, holding a hand over it or placing it between the palms whilst it is, of course, carefully shielded from the light in a black envelope, box or dark slide. Thoughtographs made in this way are called skotographs and have been produced by many photographic mediums.

Many well known psychic photographers also produced thoughtographs and skotographs during the course of their experiments and the ectoplasmic rods and flares of intense light recorded on spirit or psychic photographs during the latter half of the 19th century often seem to fall into one or the other of these categories, being produced by the will or conscious effort of the medium rather than by discarnate spirits or entities. It has even been suggested that, in many cases, the shrouded and veiled figures surrounded by cotton wool-like ectoplasmic clouds that so often appeared in their photographs were, in reality, the typical mental images created by the religious beliefs and Spiritualist outlook of that time.

In his paper 'ESP and memory' published in the *International Journal of Neuro-psychiatry* Vol 2, 1966, pages 505-21, W.G. Roll suggested that one of the reasons for the apparent following of fads and fashions in supernormal phenomena in general is because these supernormal talents may well operate in the physical world by exciting the appropriate memory traces in the medium and so the phenomena often appear to run in cycles of similarities. Even the most talented possessors of super-normal powers often show a lack of control over them that can only be compared with the lack of control that a baby has over its limbs.

In many of Mumler's psychic photographs the extra images which were obtained were so much like the people that sitters had in mind that, at one time, rather than accepting the factuality of his talent it was seriously suggested that he was employing men to break into the homes of people who had visited his studio in order to steal photographs of their deceased relatives which he then used to produce the extra images in his psychic photographs.

Photographers who have obtained supernormal photographs have often had other supernormal talents ranging from dowsing to psychometry. For example, Edward Wyllie, a renowned American psychic photographer, was a highly regarded psychometrist who was able to combine both of his talents and produce psychic photographs or thoughtographs with recognisable extra images of people who had passed away using only some personal items that had belonged to them or, sometimes, just a lock of their hair.

Commandant Darget, an officer in the French Army in the 1890s, tried to photograph the psychic force fields that some sensitives are able to see as an aura of light around both animal and plant life. Although he did not show much evidence of having photographed this life force he was more successful with a subsequent set of experiments in which he attempted to transfer thoughts and images directly on to photographic plates, producing several successful thoughtographs using a brandy bottle as a target for the image.

There have been many scientific investigations into thoughtography since the 1860s, some under the auspices of the Society for Psychical Research and others conducted by organisations ranging from the *Daily Mail* to Harry Price's National Laboratory of Psychical Research and various universities and private experimenters. Results have been as varied as the investigators themselves. The *Daily Mail* Spirit Photography Commission, which met for the first time at the Royal Photographic Society's headquarters on November 4 1908, was composed of three Spiritualists, three well known photographic chemical and technical experts and Mr T. Thorne Baker who was watching the work of the Commission on behalf of the *Daily Mail.* Mr A.P. Sinnett, who was one of the members of the Commission, described in a

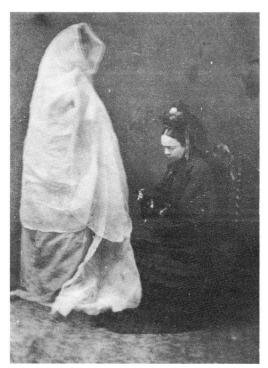

Lady Helena Newenham and the spirit of her daughter. Photograph by Frederick A. Hudson June 4 1872.

letter dated September 1 1910 how, when he was photographed by Mr Boursnell the psychic photographer, he had taken with him a new packet of plates which he had himself purchased at a randomly chosen shop, opened it in the darkroom and put one of the plates into a dark slide, himself closely examining the camera before loading it, and how after the photograph had been taken he had gone back with Boursnell into the darkroom and watched the plate being developed. He said: 'The camera which I have examined was certainly free from tricks—I do not see how I could have been cheated under these conditions'. But despite the vast quantity of evidence of this nature which was submitted to the Commission they could not come to an agreed decision on the validity of the phenomena they were investigating.

Supernormal photography is the study of people who have the ability to put psychic and mental images on to the sensitive photographic emulsion and is an attempt to discover the methods and abilities that they use for this purpose. It is sometimes an eye-opener to discover that the everyday laws of photography do not always apply and that although, in some cases, the extra images which appear in the photographs exist in reality, in others they come as if they were telepathically imprinted from someone's mind. Parapsychologists know that our minds produce images and that unusually talented people can project these images telepathically into other people's minds. It has now been shown that in special cases these images can be captured on photographic film.

Researchers at The Maimonides Dream Laboratory attached to the Department of Psychiatry of the Maimonides Medical Centre in Brooklyn, New York, which was renamed the Division of Parapsychology and Psychophysics in 1973, have conducted many series of tests designed to prove that such telepathic communication is possible and that thoughts can be communicated to someone who is asleep so that their dreams are affected and reflect the thoughts of the sender. Although the pictures and messages which are conveyed to the dreamer often appear as vague and distorted imagery in the dream, many cases of close resemblance between the target and dream have been recorded. These records show that although the best results are often obtained when the sender and dreamer are both male and the lowest score of similarities when they are both female, very good results are often obtained when the sender is female and the dreamer male. It would be interesting if the best of these senders were to try to impress the image or idea on to a photographic film or paper placed next to the dreamer.

People with the ability to project their thoughts on to photographic film have so far been few and far between but this is perhaps because few have tried to attempt it and, although the pictures which have been obtained are often fuzzy and incomplete, the important thing to remember is that it is *possible* to produce them and that with sufficient effort you, too, may be able to make thoughtographs. I know of one man who was afraid of ghosts, refused to have anything to do with Spiritualists or Spiritualism in any form, and who had a horror of seances and yet who, when tested, showed definite signs of psychic ability. In one experiment he held a pile of negative photographic plates between his hands in front of his solar plexus and, when developed, they showed signs of exposure which were graded from pronounced markings on the ones nearest to his left hand to lesser markings on those near to his right hand.

D. Scott Rogo, the well known author, describes in his book *Phantoms*, published by David and Charles, how he witnessed the production of another unexpected skotograph. Together with Raymond Bayless and von Szalay he watched as

Michaela Kelly was hypnotised for an impromptu experiment in supernormal photography. While hypnotised her hand was placed on a piece of enlarging paper. The inexplicable result was a photograph of a cartoonish picture of an aged female face with a shawl dangling behind it and the letters N A D quite clearly shown on the cloth. When Miss Kelly was re-awakened she was astounded by the photograph and said that although she had not been consciously thinking of her she had indeed once had a housekeeper named Naddie who always wore a shawl but that she had been dead for 15 years. Many researchers have reported such thoughtographs and they have been made both with and without cameras on a great variety of films and plates under many different conditions and circumstances.

Dr Baraduc experimented with supernormal photography in France in 1896. His subjects would be given a photographic plate from a new unopened box to hold in their hands and asked to concentrate a thought on to it. After developing the plate they discovered that in many cases images were to be seen. During some of these experiments the plates were sealed in black envelopes and in others the plate and subject were placed in different rooms. Baraduc found that, although very few people were able to produce this effect at a distance, the plates would occasionally show that they had been subjected to some unknown psychic influence.

Other experiments involved giving extra-long exposures in red light which should theoretically have produced no image at all. However, many of these showed swirling streams of minute luminous dots the design and location of which he was convinced varied according to the thoughts or emotions of the sitter. Similar effects which he interpreted as being the reflection of the person's physical condition were obtained when he placed a plate close to the affected part of a sick subject.

At that time, when the invention of the Crookes tube, the discovery of radium and new extentions of the photographic process were stirring people's minds, the Society for Psychical Research in London, the *Laboratoire de Physiologie des Sensations* in Paris and the American Society for Psychical Research were all encouraging scientific investigations into thoughtography and all forms of super-normal photography and eager experimenters were carrying out research projects all over the world.

In Japan thoughtography was first brought into prominence in 1910 when Professor Tomokichi Fukurai conducted a series of tests with clairvoyant mediums

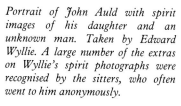

Portrait of John Auld with spirit images of his daughter and an unknown man. Taken by Edward Wyllie. A large number of the extras on Wyllie's spirit photographs were recognised by the sitters, who often went to him anonymously.

to see if they could detect the latent image on an exposed but undeveloped photographic plate. After the experimental session was concluded Fukurai discovered that the medium had created a mental image on an unexposed plate that had not been part of the original experiment and subsequent experiments showed that the medium could consistently impress such mental images on to photographic plates. The experiments with latent images and many others of a similar nature that were carried out in 1910 and 1911 by Professor Fukurai, who was described as Doctor of Literature, Professor at Kohyassan University, and President of the Psychical Institute of Japan, are described in his book *Clairvoyance and Thoughtography*, published in England by Rider and Company in 1931, and provide us with a lead to a new theory of supernormal photography and the interaction of mind and matter.

When a photograph is taken a latent image is created in the emulsion of the negative and it was this latent image that Fukurai's psychics were trying to detect. The chemical developers used by photographers reduce the suspension of silver salts in the emulsion of unexposed films or plates to metallic silver very slowly but the creation of a latent image by exposure to even a minute amount of light causes a chemical change in the crystals which increases the rate of reduction of the grains of silver halides to silver by a hundredfold. During more than a century of investigation we have discovered much of what is involved in the creation of this latent image but many of the most important facts still puzzle scientists today. What is known is that when the development of the photographic emulsion is observed through a powerful microscope, whilst the unexposed grains show no change at all the development of the exposed grains starts at only one or two points on the surface of each grain even though the whole of the grain has been exposed to light. Further investigation by chemists and physicists has shown that these starting points on each exposed grain of emulsion are triggered by the action of light which causes some of the bromide ions in the silver bromide grains of the emulsion to eject electrons. Because of their minute proportions and delicate balance it is probably these minuscule subatomic energy flows that are influenced in thoughtography and most other types of supernormal photography. The latent sub-image is also the possible starting point of some types of supernormal photographs.

Images are sometimes so lightly impressed on the film that modern development techniques do not bring them out. In the earlier days of photography, however, when plates and even films were individually developed by hand until an image was seen, rather than by the modern time and temperature methods, it may well have been this prolongation of development until the latent sub-image was seen that brought out the extra images in the photograph and this provides an interesting field of experiment for the dedicated researcher.

The action of the human will upon matter in delicately balanced solutions was shown over 50 years ago by Dr Littlefield of Seattle, USA, and is one of the phenomena which Arthur Conan Doyle investigated during his visit to the United States in 1923 and recorded in his book *Our Second American Adventure*. Dr Littlefield had studied the work of a farmer who could stop bleeding in men or animals solely by willing this to happen. He came to the conclusion that this healing power acted on the saline constituents of the blood and experimented with these salts, which include sulfates and chlorides of potassium and sodium, with amazing results. When a saturated solution of any one of these salts in distilled water is allowed to dry out naturally on a glass slide it will always show the same type of crystaline formation. The microscopic crystals have a standard shape and arrangement for each different salt. Dr Littlefield found, however, that if they were influenced whilst they were still drying out the crystals would arrange themselves into almost any pattern or shape that his mind directed. He found that he did not have to stay next to the slide to produce this result and that distance made no difference to the effect produced, which leads us to suspect that he was endowed with some personal psychic talent as we know the effects of psychic phenomena, unlike those of ordinary electromagnetic radiation, are not diluted by distance.

The pictures produced by Dr Littlefield were microscopic and he preserved his results by taking photomicrographs of a great number of them. He made many more experiments of this type and found that the salts would sometimes apparently answer questions by giving strange and seemingly meaningful diagrams in reply. There seems to be no doubt that Dr Littlefield could in some way cause images to appear in crystalising salt solutions and it is a pity that it did not occur to him to try to influence the delicately balanced photographic emulsion directly.

Dr Littlefield's work has been born out more recently by Professor Dr N. van Dorp van Vliet, DSc, DLitt, who is the Principal of the *Nederlanse Biologische Stichting* in Holland and a member of the New York Academy of Science, the Institute of Nuclear Energy, University of Stuttgart, the London Institute of Nuclear Engineers and many other academic societies. In his paper 'The Crystallisation of Radionic Frequencies' which he later retitled 'The Crystallisation of *Magnetic* Frequencies', and read at the annual meeting of the Radionic Centre Organisation on October 18 1969, he told how the experiments that both he and the late George de la Warr had conducted showed that micro-magnetic frequencies and the amplitudes emitted from audio-sonic magnetic instruments could affect mineral salts and organic substances and how this substantiated George de la Warr's theories of the existence and detection of radionic energy.

In his first prototype radionic camera de la Warr obtained images from crystals rotated to their critical rotational position in the Earth's magnetic field and focused on to X-ray plates by a radionic energy collector. However, Professor van Dorp van Vliet obtained his results without using a camera at all by transmitting a predetermined range of magnetic frequency patterns including audio-sound wave oscillations through saturated solutions of various metalic salts.

'We know,' he wrote, 'that each particular salt may have a different crystalline shape of its own. But also typical minute crystalline images, variable and specific according to the dial settings and turning of the magnetic instruments, have become manifest with this process now enabling me to make further interpretation and/or progressive analysis.'

An abridgement of his speech in the winter 1969-70 News Letter of the Radionic Centre Organisation is illustrated with a number of photographs which show that whilst, for example, a pure saturated solution of $FeSO_4$ has a clearly recognisable pattern of crystallisation, this pattern is altered if the saturated solution is irridated by magnetic wave forms whilst it is crystallising and that each different type of irridation creates its own distinct pattern of crystallisation.

He wrote, '. . . we may also assume that transmission of these elusive energies in pattern form do not require any special state of "rapport" . . . no one has yet been able to replicate these experiments which in itself suggests that some psychic talent was involved in the production of the variant images'.

Similar experiments to those conducted by Professor Fukurai are now being carried on by the Japanese Nengraphy Association, nengraphy being the Japanese

name for thoughtography, and considerable success has been achieved by the association which now has several hundred members. A well illustrated book, *Present-Day Nengraphy (thoughtography) and its experimental Demonstration*, written in Japanese by Tsutoma Miyauchi was published in 1972 describing the work of the association and the progress of thoughtography and psychic photography in Japan since it was brought into prominence again by the establishment of a new group the *Jikido-kai*, in Kobe, by Mr Jikido Tatsumi. It gives details of experiments carried out by Miyauchi with many psychics and supernormal photographers. In one series of experiments Miyauchi sent fresh sheets of film sealed in light-proofed containers to a number of groups and individual thoughtographers all over Japan with many interesting results which are reproduced in his book. Taimei Shigenaga, Utako Tanimiyu and five other members of the *Jikido-kai* produced positive results by creating mental cloud-like images and bursts of light on their films and these, together with the work of 68 other members of the club which by then had a total membership of about 260, are illustrated in the book.

Cloudy markings were also produced mentally on film by a Mr Shakujinen, a thoughtographer who was a member of the Shingon, a Mahayana Buddhist sect, who had become well known for his brilliant thoughtography published in 1970 and members of the Institute for Research of Hypnology in Nara, Japan, produced thoughtographs whilst in a deep hypnotic trance and even more amazingly some of them showed that they were able to remove the latent image from an exposed film by mental concentration alone so that it returned to its original imageless unexposed state.

The association has also published three important reports on their investigations in thoughtography, PK Report No 1 *Practical Studies of Nengraphical Phenomena (The Studies of Nengraphy by Masuaki Kiyota)*, edited by Tsutomu Miyauchi, member of JNA, J. Tsunado and Y. Kiyota; PK Report No 2 *Physical Studies of Nengraphical and Nenelectrical Phenomena* by T. Miyauchi and Y. Fukuda, both

Left *This portrait of John Mercer by Edward Wyllie, taken in 1895, has extra psychic images of his mother, his first wife and a spirit message.*

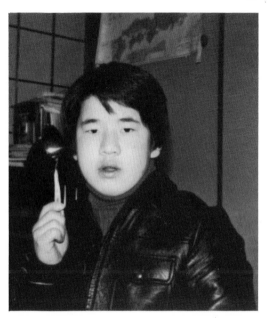

Right *Masuaki Kiyota demonstrating the paranormal twisting of a spoon on December 27 1975 (courtesy of Toshihiko Ichimura).*

members of the JNA, and PK Report No 3 *Mathematical Studies of Nengraphical and Nenelectrical Phenomena* by T. Miyauchi; the first two of these are also illustrated with many actual thoughtographs.

The Director of the Japanese Parapsychological Research Association, Toshihiko Ichimura, is also the editor of the magazine *Telepathy* which has reported much of the Japanese work on supernormal photography including the more than 300 experiments conducted by Tsutomu Miyauchi with the Japanese teenage psychic wonder Masuaki Kiyota, who has shown that he has the ability to transmit mental images on to unexposed film under rigid scientific conditions. Professor Shigemi Sasaki of the University of Electro-Communications at Chofu, near Toyko, and Yugi Ogawa of the Nippon Electric Company, Tamagawa, published a scientific paper *Some Experimental Studies on the Appearance of Nenography (Thoughtography) by Psychokinesis*, on Kiyota's supernormal talents. This paper compared the results obtained in the experiments conducted with him by T. Miyauchi and Y. Fukuda in 1975 and 1976 and published in January 1977 as the JNA PK Report No 2 with the similar investigations of the thoughtographic abilities of Kiyota and several other subjects carried out in their laboratory during the same period in an attempt to discover the fundamental nature of the experimental results.

For one of their most interesting experiments they removed the lens and the front part of a Polaroid camera, placed light-sensitive silicone diodes just above the film in the back and covered them with a light-proof paper seal. When the medium focused his thoughts on the Polaroid film the light-sensitive diodes recorded inexplicable electronic disturbances on a sensitive graph penrecorder and similar results were obtained in a lightproof sealed steel box.

Dr Walter Uphoff and his wife Mary Jo, authors of *New Psychic Frontiers*, Colin Smythe Limited, 1975, also supervised a series of experiments with Kiyota under laboratory conditions in Tokyo and were convinced of the lad's amazing paranormal powers. Professor Uphoff, who was lecturer in parapsychology at the University of

Above *Group spirit photograph by Mrs Ada Deane.*

Left *On the back of this photograph is the handwritten statement: 'On the other side is a portrait of my cousin recognised by all whom we know as capable of recognising her, and who passed on ten years before the portrait was taken. The sitter, you will see, is myself.' Signed, J. Dixon MD 59 Great Ormond St, London. Photograph taken by Frederick A. Hudson, November 1872.*

Above right *Energy can be seen building up over the congregation in this psychic photograph taken by Mrs Ada Deane on November 11 1932.*

Colorado, also conducted experiments with Kiyota in the United States for a special NBC-TV programme on paranormal phenomena. For one of these experiments a loaded Polaroid camera, which the young man had not seen before, was placed on the table in front of him. Although the lens cap was in place over the lens and the shutter release was not touched, by concentrating his thoughts upon the film he produced photographs which showed an aerial view of a nearby hotel, the Tokyo Tower, and other astounding images.

Kiyota was also successful in tests conducted for Granada TV during his visit to England in August 1978. He was flown to Manchester by the TV company which had planned a special feature programme on which he could demonstrate his supernormal talents. Gordon Burns, the presenter, in an interview reported in the *Sun* newspaper said that Kiyota produced some bent forks during tests for psychokinesis and the 'Geller' effect and, by concentrating for a few seconds, produced thoughtographs on the film in a sealed Polaroid camera.

Sadar Nakamichi, vice-president of the Japan Nengraphy Association, and his assistant, Yukio Ishii, another pair of visitors to Great Britain in 1978, have also shown their ability to produce thoughtographs on the film in sealed Polaroid cameras and several Japanese psychic mediums have recently demonstrated this ability to transfer thought images on to film.

Professor Fukurai held that spirit photography—the photographic recording of the images of people who had passed away from this life—and thoughtography—the creation of mental photographic images by the living—were manifestations of the same talent and that spirit photography mediums should also be able to produce thoughtographs. In order to support this conclusion, when his sittings with spirit photographers were concluded he always tried to take a thoughtograph with the same medium. During his visit to William Hope in Crew on September 29 1928,

This unusual thoughtograph was made by medium Madge Donohue without the use of a camera.

Fukurai conducted in this way two successful tests for thoughtography. Having signed his name in Japanese characters on each plate, and with his friend Yamamoto standing beside Hope and carefully watching every movement, Fukurai insisted that these photographs were completely genuine and indeed he achieved similar positive results using similar methods with many different mediums.

Many other mediums were also producing thoughtographs at this time. One of these was Madge Donohue, a remarkable photographic medium who produced thousands of thoughtographs without using a camera at all. For 20 years, from 1920 until she passed away in 1940, she produced them regularly by placing unexposed photographic plates protected in light proof envelopes under her pillow before retiring at night and sleeping on them. Madge Donohue was a sincere Spiritualist. This may have influenced the fact that many of the pictures received were of people who had passed away whilst others contained messages which also came from deceased people. Her constant prayers for evidence of life after death were further answered by one series of 140 thoughtographs received in this way over a seven-month period which contained messages telling the supposed life story of King Amon, a Pharaoh of ancient Egypt, and another series of more than 300 thoughto-graphs which told the story of the golden age of Greece in pictures and messages. On several occasions, however, the images which appeared were photographs of living people and large numbers of them had pictures of a vase of flowers sent to her by her dead husband. There were nearly a thousand of these and no two of them were exactly the same.

Mrs Ada Deane, another successful psychic photographer who became prominent in Britain after the First World War, produced many thoughtographs as well as large numbers of spirit photographs which showed extra images of people who had passed away from this life superimposed either on the portraits of the sitters or on the background behind them. Her spirit photographs included a well known series taken on successive anniversaries of Armistice Day which showed extra images of many soldiers who had died during the war. Although the authenticity of Mrs Deane's spirit photographs was challenged and, like other psychic photographers

Armistice Day photograph, 1924, taken by Mrs Ada Deane.

she was at times accused of fraud, many contemporary researchers disputed these accusations and vouched for her honesty. A number of psychic researchers conducted successful experiments with her and showed conclusively that Mrs Deane did in fact produce successful psychic photographs and thoughtographs. One of these, the seasoned American psychic investigator Hereward Carrington, reported a series of carefully controlled experiments during 1925, using specially prepared and marked plates, on many of which Mrs Deane impressed inexplicable mental images, blurs and columns of light. Other equally distinguished authorities also witnessed her production of supernormal photographs.

There have been as many different methods used to produce thoughtographs as there have been thoughtographs themselves and successful ones have been produced by young and old, men and women of all nationalities and beliefs since the early 1860s.

Writing in the British Edition of *Fate* magazine, in June 1976, Margaret E.W. Fleming told of her 20 years' experience in the making of what she called 'spirit pictures', several of which are preserved in the Library of Special Collections at the University of Colorado. Working in a darkened room she holds a sheet of ordinary photographic paper to her forehead and concentrates her thoughts on the image she wants to produce. When she feels that the image is sufficiently impressed she holds the paper on the palm of her hand with the emulsion side up and gives it a brief one-second exposure to the white light of a 60-Watt lamp, rinses it under running water for a short while and plunges it into a tray of developer in which she leaves it until an image appears. When she is successful in the production of a thoughtograph she says the image appears fairly quickly and when it can be clearly seen she removes the paper from the developer, rinses it and puts it into a tray of hypo fixing solution for ten minutes, and then washes it well in running water for an hour to remove as much of the remaining chemicals as possible. This is a simple, standard way of developing the resulting photographs, which anyone can use, but longer and more permanent methods can be found in any photographic textbook and supplementary chemical baths and prolonged washing times can be used to give more permanence to the picture.

Ted Serios, one of the best investigated and most prolific thoughtographers of recent years, used a Polaroid Land camera to record the projected patterns of his thoughts and with it he has produced hundreds of thoughtographs which cover the entire gamut of photographic images from prints which are entirely black to ones which are entirely white and to pictures of far off people and places. In his book on Serios Dr Jule Eisenbud, a Denver psychiatrist and associate professor of Colorado Medical School, told how he (Serios) began experimenting with hypnosis with a fellow employee, Mr George Johannes, whilst they were working at the Conrad Hilton Hotel in Chicago and how they discovered that Serios was an excellent subject who could easily be directed to see far away places and people whilst in an hypnotic trance. This type of 'travelling clairvoyance' was noted in some of Mesmer's earliest experiments with 'animal magnetism' or 'mesmerism' and, in Serios' case, it was suggested that he travelled for a while with Jean Laffite the notorious pirate who was pardoned by President Madison after fighting with the United States in the Battle of New Orleans in 1815. After Jean Laffite had 'shown' Serios various places where he had supposedly hidden his pirate treasure, Johannes began directing Ted Serios to go treasure-hunting in and around Chicago itself in the hope of obtaining some tangible results from their experiments. After some successful but small results Johannes suggested that Ted could possibly get more details of what he claimed he was 'seeing' if he could project it on film and he loaned Ted a sealed camera with which to try. When the film was returned from the processors with a couple of pictures on it Ted bought a camera of his own and was baffled by the results that he obtained. In order to make sure that the pictures were not being caused by accident or error in the processing he began using a Polaroid camera so that he could see his results almost immediately with no possibility of outside intervention. At first he tried pointing the camera at a wall about a foot away but, after many months of making these pictures with no return in treasure, he became ill and, acting on the advice of a psychiatrist, stopped his experiments and did not touch a camera for nearly 18 months until, haunted by the seeming success of some of his photographs, he went to a professional hypnotist and was soon taking his mental photographs again. This hypnotist suggested that Ted tried pointing the

Dr John J. Conger, Dean of the University of Colorado Medical School, had the palm of his hand flat over the gismo that Ted Serios was holding when he produced this thoughtograph of a double-decker bus (courtesy of Jule Eisenbud MD).

camera at himself whilst in a hypnotic trance but, after a while, he found that the hypnosis became ineffectual and that he could only take the thought pictures whilst he was in his normal waking state.

At times Ted finds it impossible to obtain pictures of any kind on the film whilst at others when he is 'hot' he is able to produce picture after picture, often of buildings but also of many other subjects. He has produced pictures with the observer's hands covering the lens of the camera and even with the lens of the camera entirely removed, and he has done so using cameras and film he had not previously seen or touched which were provided by independent witnesses. The fact that Ted Serios almost invariably directs his thoughts on to the film using what he calls a 'gismo' held between this thumb and forefinger and placed against he tube of the camera often causes comment. Ted's gismo is a small tube about 1 or 2 cm long with the ends sometimes covered with pieces of blackened film or cellophane. The tube itself is made of plastic or cardboard, sometimes it is merely a 1 or 2 cm length cut from the plastic tube that holds the squeegee used for fixing the Polaroid prints after they are developed or even a piece of the black paper from a Polaroid film pack wrapped around to make an open-ended tube. Ted said that he started using these devices to keep his fingers away from the camera lens and to cut down the amount of light entering the camera and that he has now got so used to them that he is uncomfortable and finds it difficult to work without one. Researchers working with Serios have, however, made a practice of thoroughly searching him and examining the gismo he was using before, during and after each session and nothing suspicious has ever been found.

Some of these thoughtographs seem to have been taken from a vantage point high up in the air and, on at least one occasion, Serios has even attempted to produce photographs of the moon and outer space. He carried out no special preparation for this thoughtography, although he often drinks a lot during the sessions, but simply concentrates on the image he wants to create, points the Polaroid camera at his face or puts it to his forehead and mentally projects the image on to the film. He can often tell when he is going to take a successful thoughtograph and has been able to produce thought photographs of target images which have been hidden in sealed opaque envelopes.

Dr Eisenbud tells me that up to the date of publication of his book Serios had been mostly using one of the Model 95 series Polaroid Land cameras set at aperture No 3, or exposure value 12 in the later models of the camera, which is the equivalent to 1/30 second at f11. A wink light, the Polaroid flash-light attachment, was usually used with it and the time exposure knob was taped over so that it could not be used and the focusing lever was set to infinity. For almost all the experiments Polaroid type 47 black and white high speed film of 3,000 ASA was used and, in most cases, this was provided by one of an impressive list of independent witnesses who loaded or supervised the loading of the camera with the film from the sealed packets which they themselves provided, all exposed prints being pulled out of the camera and developed in the presence of the witnesses.

If you have, or can obtain, a Polaroid camera it would be well worth while trying to duplicate some of these experiments and seeing if you can also produce thoughtographs. Although the prices of Polaroid film today makes these experiments expensive, they do provide the great satisfaction and encouragement of producing immediate results and, should any of these results be positive, it will of course make the whole thing worth while. It is possible to buy slightly outdated packs of Polaroid

films at greatly reduced prices. These are quite satisfactory for our purposes and will greatly reduce the cost of experiments. These remarks apply equally to the Kodak instant cameras and films which, although involving a different internal chemistry to the Polaroid process, give results which are sufficiently similar for our purposes.

It has been suggested that the thoughtographs produced by Ted Serios can be faulted because, in a number of cases, he had the opportunity of handling the film pack or the camera or because he held a gismo in front of the lens even though, as we have seen, this was a simple device having no sinister uses. Although it is, of course, possible to produce an extraneous image by holding a small lens covered with a transparency in front of the camera lens, this can in no way reproduce the results obtained by Ted Serios under rigorous test conditions which include producing thoughtographs that closely correspond to target ideas or images which were carefully kept from him until immediately before the thoughtograph was taken and his complete separation from the camera before during and after the taking of the photograph and the processing of the film. He has produced dozens and dozens of thoughtographs, at distances ranging from 1 to 60 ft from the camera, whilst being continuously monitored and observed by competent scientific investigators, and many of these pictures have been recognised as reasonable images of the target. At times he has even produced thoughtographs with one investigator holding the camera, a second holding a gismo in front of the lens and a third triggering the shutter.

The evaluation of the relationship between some of the thoughtographs and the original target pictures that Ted was trying for has also been criticised, but nevertheless there remains a hard core of genuinely inexplicable thoughtographs which could not have been produced by any of the normal photographic methods or by almost any conceivable kind of trickery. Photographs have been produced using cameras and film which had been supplied by unimpeachable independent witnesses who held the camera, covered the lens with their hands and tripped the shutter themselves, so that Ted could have in no way physically influenced the

Right *Spirit photograph by Mrs Ada Deane.*

resulting photographs, at times with the entire experiment being filmed to ensure that later inspection would again confirm that no trickery of any kind was involved, and upon occasion even with the camera in the room and Ted in an entirely different rooms some 30 ft away.

Scientific tests have failed to show how Ted Serios produces his thoughtographs. Dr Eisenbud has reported that nothing of significance was revealed when Serios produced thoughtographs whilst being monitored with an electroencephalograph and that he could produce pictures whilst in a $2 \times 3 \times 2\frac{1}{2}$ m high doubly screened copper mesh Faraday cage and that he was even successful when the film was protected by a $\frac{1}{16}$-inch lead lined container.

Blindfolding Ted Serios also makes no difference to his ability to produce these thoughtographs and, although he almost always used a loaded Polaroid camera in his experiments, he has occasionally produced pictures on a non-exposed Polaroid film pack and has been able to get images on the film when the camera was being held by someone else behind a partition some distance away. Many of the scientists who investigated his ability to project thought images on to Polaroid film brought their own cameras and films with them to preclude any suggestion of trickery and, in the course of several years of scientific experiments and strictly controlled tests, he successfully produced thoughtographs using several different models of the Polaroid Land camera with several different types of film pack including the type 413 infra-red film.

Thoughtographs produced by Ted Serios include images of subjects ranging from an Air Force manned orbiting laboratory in space, Big Ben, the Chicago Hilton Hotel, a double-decker bus, the Eiffel Tower, an Olmec stele, the Opera House at Central City, Colorado, Her Majesty Queen Elizabeth II and the late President Kennedy to the White House and Westminster Abbey. The completely black or completely white Polaroid pictures which he has produced on many occasions are as mysterious as his pictorial thoughtographs. A Polaroid film which comes out all white with no picture showing after processing can only be produced by exposing the film to a bright light source, by photographing a well illuminated plain white sheet or screen, or by grossly over exposing the film. It cannot normally be made, as Ted has done, by taking an ordinary self-portrait of his face in ordinary room lighting. Completely black prints which should have, of course, shown something of Ted's face, are just as unusual and exciting and seem just as impossible to produce in any ordinary way. Ted seems to create a mental barrier which stops all traces of light passing through the lens on to the film.

In a paper 'A physical analysis of the psychic photography of Ted Serios' by R. Giles of the Department of Mathematics, Queens University, Kingston, Ontario, Canada, published in Volume 1, No 2 of the *Journal of Research into Psi Phenomena*, 1976, the author suggested that the supernormal effects produced by Ted Serios create a limited 'disturbed region' of space/time and that the type of supernormal photographs produced, that is all white, all black or with supernormal images, depends on the positioning of this limited supernormal disturbed region with respect to the camera. The all white photographs seem to be produced when the disturbed region is created inside the camera thus flooding the film with light. Supernormal images are produced when the disturbed region is created just outside the camera in front of the lens. All black photographs are made by the same mechanism that blacks out the normal image which would otherwise be super-imposed on a supernormal photograph. This differs from the photographs and thoughtographs taken by many other supernormal photographers who do not seem able to black out the background in their photographs and usually produce a super-normal image superimposed on the normal view of the background which is recorded at the same time.

Dr J.G. Pratt and Dr Ian Stevenson conducted a series of experiments under carefully controlled conditions with Ted Serios at the University of Virginia at Charlottesville during April and May 1967. The researchers supplied the cameras and films which they and their collaborators and assistants kept under continual scrutiny and they chose the target images themselves. Even under these rigorous

Bob Brown, train robber, from Gunfighters of the West, *by Ed Bartholomew. In this, the only known published photograph of Bob Brown, his eyes are open whilst in the Veilleux supernormal portrait his eyes are closed* (courtesy of the Veilleux family).

Bob Brown, Train Robber

Bob Brown, shown at left was a member of the gang which attempted to rob the El Paso and Southwestern passenger train at Fairbanks, Arizona, February 20, 1900, but were unsuccessful. In the fight between the robbers and Jeff D. Milton, the express messenger, Milton was shot in the left arm, and John Patterson, alias Dunlap, alias Three-Fingered Jack, was killed. The other members of the gang, which included the Owens brothers, Lewis and George, Bob Brown and Matt Burts, were all eventually run to earth and captured, and all of them were convicted and served long terms in the Arizona State penitentiary at Yuma. When Bob Brown was released from prison he dropped out of sight, and nothing was ever heard from him again.

test conditions Serios was able to produce thoughtographs of images and scenes several of which were recognised.

The 'decline effect', the tailing off of positive results in both individual experiments and in the continuing work of any successful psychic which is familiar to all parapsychologists, was by now becoming apparent to those working with Serios. This series of experiments ended a month earlier than was expected when Ted became unhappy with the tailing off of successful results which seemed to be taking place and returned to his home in Chicago. Although some successful thoughtographs were produced on Polaroid films during a second series of experiments at the University of Virginia in 1968 nothing at all was produced during a third series in 1969 when Serios gave up the attempts after three days. His psychic talent seemed to taper right off after this and, although he kept on trying to produce psychic pictures with several different cameras, his talent remained dormant for years until the public clamour and interest in the case of Patricia Hearst the kidnapped heiress excited him and encouraged him to try to obtain a psychic photograph of her. After experimenting for more than a year and taking over a hundred photographs with this Polaroid 3000 camera, he finally came up with a photograph which he claimed showed Patricia Hearst in front of a large San Fransisco hotel and, soon after this, he made three more photographs of an unidentified short-haired young woman on an otherwise blank film exposed on Instamatic Model 110 camera he had borrowed from his mother. He used this camera in his usual fashion with a flashgun attached and just pointing it towards himself and made a flash exposure when he felt that the moment was right. Neither the Hearst family, to whom Serios sent a copy of the first of these photographs, nor the Federal Bureau of Investigation who saw the later ones, would confirm that they were photographs of the missing heiress or take any further action about them, although it did later transpire that by then Patricia Hearst had indeed had her hair cut short.

Serios has not produced any significant thoughtographs since and his talent seems to have disappeared entirely, although he still makes spasmodic attemtps to rekindle

Supernormal photograph taken by the Veilleux family in June 1968. Identified by Dr Jule Eisenbud in 1969 as Bob Brown. Internationally copyrighted by the Veilleux family, 1974, and reproduced with their permission.

it. It was he, however, who brought Willi Schwanholz, another talented producer of paranormal photographs, to the public's notice. Schwanholz, a Canadian citizen of German origin, had many psychic experiences and on three occasions has inexplicably appeared on Super 8 ciné films taken by friends in Germany whilst he himself was in the United States. He has successfully recorded supernormal voices on tape replicating the pioneering work of Friedrich Juergeson in Sweden in 1959, and Dr Konstantin Raudive in Germany in 1965 and, in addition to unknown voices similar to those recorded by Juergeson and Dr Raudive, Schwanholz has recorded voices which seem to be of people watching his every action and movement in the room.

Schwanholz heard of Ted Serios' thoughtographs in January 1976 and, convinced that if he could appear on a ciné film taken when he was not present he would also be able to take psychic photographs himself, traced Serios' home address, called and introduced himself. Serios showed him how he held the Polaroid camera pointed to his face and held the gismo in front of the lens and Schwanholz was almost immediately successful in obtaining extra images on the Polaroid prints. Schwanholz has taken many supernormal photographs since then, including a spectacular series of seven thoughtographs of young women in swim suits and bikinis and two extra-ordinary ones that were shown to me by Professor Walter Uphoff when he visited my office, whilst he was in England last year, which seem to be photographs of twisted strips of motion picture films against a dark background, one showing a series of head and shoulder photographs of a young girl and the other what appears to be groups of marching soldiers.

Professor Uphoff, who conducted an honours course 'Developments in Parapsychology' at the University of Colorado and has been conducting research in the field of psychic phenomena in general and supernormal photography in particular for many years, is one of a number of researchers who have studied the thoughtographs and other mental and psychic phenomena which seem to centre on Schwanholz.

Both Dr Eisenbud and Professor Uphoff have also investigated the supernormal Polaroid pictures that the Veilleux family in Waterville, Miane, USA, have been producing since 1867. Like many others before them the Veilleux family, Mrs Joseph and Mrs Violet Veilleux, two married sons Fred and Richard and their wives, began to toy with a Ouija board almost as a joke, but they soon began to receive messages through it and, as these messages gradually grew more coherent, the Veilleux became more and more interested and involved with their experiments. They started using the Ouija board in 1966 and, on the evening of August 1 1977, they received a message telling them to load their Polaroid camera with film point it at the blank wall of the room and take a photograph. Following the instructions, but still in a disbelieving mood, they took a photograph as the message had suggested and were astonished to find the face of a young girl surrounded by a whitish cloud on the finished print. They immediately recognised her as a neighbour's dead child. Convinced of the authenticity of the messages and the instructions which they were receiving via the Ouija board they took more photographs in the same way until, in the course of time, they had a number of these supernormal photographs with unusual images and strange faces on them. In June 1968, acting on the advice of the American Society for Psychical Research, Richard Veilleux wrote to Dr Jule Eisenbud asking for his opinion of their photographs and his advice on the methods they were using to take them. Coming, as it did, at the time when Ted Serios'

Phantom energy patterns persist even after the leaves are entirely removed from the stems. Left the ghost leaves can be seen; right one of a series of controls (courtesy of Harry Oldfield).

thoughtography had almost completely faded away the letter was welcome news and, in September 1968, Dr Eisenbud called on the Veilleux family in Waterville to conduct experiments with them himself. After several blank sessions they went to the local cemetery, where the Veilleux had previously taken successful supernormal photographs. Using the Ouija board on the back seat of the car Richard and Fred received a message claiming to come from a William D. Gittings who said that he had hanged himself when he was 13 years old and that, if they would take photographs of his grave, something unusual would happen.

Loading his Model 100 Polaroid camera, Dr Eisenbud handed it to Fred Veilleux and watched carefully as he pointed it at the little flat stone grave marker which read simply 'William D. Gittings, 1943-1956'. Working under Dr Eisenbud's constant supervision Fred Veilleux took several photographs of the little grave. The first four of these were quite ordinary but the fifth photograph certainly was unusual with most of the image whitened out and the left edge covered with mottled markings. Eisenbud met the male members of the Veilleux family again during their two-week visit to Denver in July 1969 and again partially bleached out photographs and photographs with cloudlike formations that seemed to be the beginnings of super-normal images were taken but nothing really recognisable was obtained.

Professor Uphoff, who spent a weekend with the Veilleux family in May 1969 investigating the anomalies that they were getting on their Polaroid pictures, also witnessed them obtaining supernormal photographs, both with their own camera and with the one which he had taken with him to their Waterville home. However, like most people who can take thoughtographs or any other kind of supernormal photographs, their ability is not constant and they have lean periods, sometimes of months or even years, during which nothing of any significance appears. One such

Left *British metal bender Stephen North created this psychokinetic paperclip sculpture. Although the 6-inch glass globe has a $\frac{1}{8}$-inch hole in the top, Professor John Hasted was convinced that there was no way in which the paperclips could have been first straightened and then intertwined by physical means.*

Below *Uri Geller (courtesy of Robson Books).*

period was from the early summer of 1972 until spring 1974 and another lasting several months occurred at the end of 1975 when Dr A.R.G. Owen reported in the December issue of the *Journal of Parapsychology* that the Toronto Society for Psychical Research, which he had been instrumental in creating, had conducted a series of experiments with Joseph, Fred and Richard Veilleux but that only minor paranormal effects were observed and no results of any great value or significance had been obtained. When the Veilleux had been in a good period, however, they have taken spectacular supernormal photographs which vie with anything produced by Serios or any other modern thoughtographer.

Although Ted Serios could often control the pictures on his thoughtographs and by concentrating fiercely enough produce a good replica of the target images set for him, the talent of the Veilleux is of a more haphazard nature and they have had little or no control over the extra images produced in their thoughtographs, although sometimes messages received via the Ouija board tell them what images to aim for or predict what will appear. In spite of this they have taken a large number of photographs which have thought images impressed on them, sometimes in addition to and sometimes instead of the conventional expected image of the person or place at which the camera was pointed.

Uri Geller is yet another psychic with the ability to superimpose inexplicable thought images on photographs. Lawrence Fried, President of the American Society of Media Photographers one of a number of leading professional photographers who have investigated Geller's thoughtographs, describes in *The Geller Papers, Scientific Observations on the Paranormal Powers of Uri Geller*, edited by Charles Panati, Houghton Mifflin Company, Boston, 1976, an example of Geller's thought photography which he personally witnessed.

Fried had secured the lens cap on to the lens of the camera with photographers' 2-inch cloth-like tape wrapped several times around the lens cap and the barrel of the lens and, whilst he watched closely, Geller just pointed the camera to his head and pressed the shutter. Although there was no way in which light could have reached the film and Fried was convinced that in the circumstances trickery could not have been involved, the resulting photograph was 'somewhat out of focus and slightly under-exposed but unmistakably a photograph of Geller'.

News of the World crack reporter Roy Stockdill and news photographer Michael Brennan, who has been awarded the title British Press Photographer of the Year, took the front page of the Sunday December 2 1973 issue of that newspaper with the picture story of their interview with Uri Geller at the Eden Roc Hotel, Miami Beach, Florida, where Geller took two thoughtograph self-portraits which they described as impossible and 'defying all laws of natural science and photography'. Under the close and constant scrutiny of these two experienced newsmen Geller took Brennan's Nikon camera, which had its lens covered by the standard Nikon lens cap that twists on to the end of the lens barrel like the lid on a jam jar and as an additional safety measure is securely held in place by two clips, and holding it at arms' length pointed it at his face and rapidly exposed three rolls of film alternately releasing the shutter and quickly winding the film on, occasionally putting the lens cap against his forehead as if he was trying to take pictures inside his head. Michael Brennan provided the film and loaded and unloaded his camera himself. Geller did not touch the films or their containers and both Stockdill and Brennan were convinced that Geller could not have taken off or even moved the lens cap in any way.

When the three rolls of film were developed, two of the films were completely blank, as was to be expected of films exposed in a camera with the lens completely covered, but in the middle of the otherwise blank third film there were two quite clear and distinct pictures of Uri Geller and the newspaper published them, together with a photograph showing Geller taking these amazing self-portraits with the lens cap in place over the lens of the camera which Brennan had taken during the experiment, on the front page to illustrate the story.

The straightforward photographing of talented people like Uri Geller whilst they are producing supernormal phenomena of any kind is also of great value, not only because of the possibility of taking an almost inadvertent supernormal photograph, but also because it allows us to re-examine the circumstances around the fleeting phenomena at our leisure and it is this which makes films such as those made during Geller's visit to the Stanford Research Institute, and the films and videotapes made during his experiments in other scientific laboratories, so important.

Professor J.B. Hasted and Professor John Taylor have both observed the inexplicable movement of objects and the affecting of a Geiger counter when Uri is attempting to create the 'Geller effect' and many other scientists and researchers of similar ability and high quality have corroborated their evidence and backed it up with film and videotape recordings.

Recent experiments in psychokinesis have shown that many people have the ability to move and manipulate small objects by an effort of will without touching them physically. The mental force that they exert in experiments when they move a box of matches or a table tennis ball or something of this nature is immeasurably greater than that necessary to cause the movement of individual electrons in a delicately balanced photographic emulsion, so people with this ability should have little difficulty in at least affecting the condition of photographic materials and, with practice and training, many could probably produce recognisable thoughtographs. This has been the case with Nina Sergeyevna Kulagina, the Soviet housewife mentioned earlier who lives with her engineer husband in Leningrad. Kulagina's talents include moving small objects ranging from matches and cigarettes to large tumblers and glass vases (at times moving different ones simultaneously), moving a compass needle and starting and stopping a small pendulum. These strange talents have been investigated by Edward Naumov, a top Russian biologist at the Moscow State University who has filmed her Geller-like abilities, and she has triumphed in tests under increasingly severe conditions imposed in government laboratories.

In one film demonstration of her psychokinetic energy Kulagina demonstrated her fine control of this talent. A raw egg was broken into a glass tank of saline solution and, whilst standing 6 ft away from the tank, she caused the white of the egg to separate and move away from the yolk and then move back and surround it again. During another series of tests, conducted this time by Dr Zdenek Rejdak, a glass bowl was filled with cigarette smoke, inverted and put upside down on to a table well away from her. Again she demonstrated her fine control of psychokinesis by separating the smoke into two halves right through the glass. She is in excellent company in the world of psychokinetic talent. Celebrated mediums like Dunglas Home, Eusapia Palladino, Stanislaw Tomczyk, Rudi Schneider and countless others have demonstrated this type of ability and it has often been suggested that this may indeed be the kind used in thoughtography and the other sorts of supernormal photography.

Kulagina has, in fact, developed her talent in this direction and has produced thoughtographs of simple patterns such as a cross and the letters A and O and, on several occasions, she has been able to impress the recognisable silhouette or outline of a target picture on to photographic materials. The Soviet scientist G.A. Sergeyev, who has also carried out such research into Kulagina's supernormal abilities, has made several interesting photographic records of the energies which she seems to use. When she has moved objects resting on unexposed photographic film in light-proof containers the films, when developed, showed markings and traces of exposure which seemed to image the actual psychokinetic movements of the objects and, when a 35 mm film in a light-proof cover was wrapped around her head whilst she was trying to move objects by mental force alone, clearly visible flashes and discharge marks were recorded although the film had not been exposed to light.

The governments of the Soviet Union and the other Eastern Bloc countries seem to take investigation into thoughtography and all kinds of supernormal photography far more seriously than our Western governments do and they are pressing on with research in directions that have so far been untried over here. One example of this is the successful production of a thoughtograph by a subject who is undergoing a vivid visual hallucination. Professor Genady Pavlovich Krochalev has been successfully obtaining thoughtographs of this kind in his laboratory in the Ural Mountains for some time by holding a negative film or plate in a sealed container in front of the eyes of the hallucinating subject.

An extention of this is an investigation into the long-held belief that the image of a murderer can be seen in his victims eyes and that this image of the last thing seen before death is persistent and only fades away gradually, so that a photograph of the retina of the dead person should be of help to the police. This theory is being taken very seriously in the Soviet Union and much experimental work is being done in this field of thought photography.

If we stare at anything for a while, and then close the eyes, it does not immediately fade from view or from our memory but remains, although sometimes reversed like a negative or in complementary colours. The Russians call this an 'after image' and report that they have captured it on film. This after image, they claim, is projected on to the film from where it persists on the retina by the optical system of the eyes and, if the experiment is successful, the circles of the pupil with the after image in them is seen on the resulting photograph.

Professor Krochalev obtained such successful photographs in 1974 and 1975 by having the subject stare at a black and white negative image, such as the picture of a woman, for 10 or 15 seconds and then turning out the light. The after image appeared before the eyes of the experimenter in the now completely darkened room and was projected on to the open 9 × 12 cm film holder and, when after six seconds the image disappeared from sight, the film holder was securely shut. In this way he obtained photographs of the after image of the woman's photograph and also other figures like a cross, circle, etc. He found that the clarity of the photographed after image depended on the distance between the film and the subject's eyes and that it worked best at a distance of between 15 and 20 cm.

Professor Krochalev has also experimented with a standard 8 mm ciné camera using black and white film exposed at 16 frames per second to take similar retinal photographs of a subject suffering from retinal hallucinations and produced a successful film showing the visual hallucination of telegraph poles that the subject was seeing.

Benson Herbert, Director of the Paraphysical Laboratory, Downton, Wiltshire, is one of a number of western researchers who are endeavouring to repeat this kind of photographic experiment. Reports of experimental supernormal photography are often published in his *International Journal of Paraphysics.* I have mentioned some of them here with Benson Herbert's kind permission as I have found the *Journal* to be full of fascinating reports of this kind.

Kirlian photography is another Russian innovation which has opened a promising field of investigation. By the end of the 19th century Dr Hypolyte Baraduc had shown that there was a connection between the human psyche and the aura shown in high voltage electrophotography, but it was not until new methods were developed by Semyon Davidovitch Kirlian, during and after the Second World War, that the possibilities were generally realised.

Kirlian photographs show an amazing aura of light around both living and inanimate objects and it is claimed that this aura is partly of non-physical origin and so can be modified by human thought. Dr Thelma Moss, who was one of the first western scientists to take successful Kirlian photographs, has shown that emotions affect the aura of light seen in these high frequency photographs. British researchers, Brian Snelgrove (who has spent several years in efforts to control the many variables involved in Kirlian photography) and Harry Oldfield (a biologist who has devoted much time to private research into cancer cell diagnosis with Kirlian apparatus and new machines of his own design), are amongst many who have demonstrated that healers and psychics can affect the Kirlian aura in a similar way.

Radionics, developed from the ancient art of dowsing, has provided us with another stimulating way of taking supernormal photographs which are modulated by the human psyche. Dowsing with divining rods, first for coal and other minerals and then for water, has been recorded since the Middle Ages and, when the pendulum came into use as a divining tool at the beginning of the 20th century, dowsing began to be used for medical diagnosis.

The invention of radionic instruments for the diagnosis of illness by Dr Albert Abrams after the First World War led to research by Dr Ruth Beynar Drown and her development of the instrument capable of obtaining radionic photographic images with which she took the first radionic photographs.

For all forms of supernormal photography a positive approach by the photographer and every one involved is of vital importance. In her book, *The theory and technique of the Drown HVR and radio-vision instruments*, Dr Drown emphasised this and stressed that the individual's own internal energy is the only force or current used in any of her instruments.

George de la Warr who, with is wife, Marjorie, and their colleague, Leonard P. Corte, developed their own radionic camera at the Delawarr Laboratories at Oxford, England, after the Second World War also found that the presence of someone with the necessary rapport with radionic photography was essential for successful results. As with all kinds of supernormal photography, this person can be the photographer, the subject or a third person but all present must have a positive approach for the attainment of positive results.

Kirlian and radionic photography are exciting extensions of the photographic process and are both influenced by the human psyche and thought processes but, as we have seen, thoughtographs can also be taken without using complicated instruments or expensive cameras.

The very variety of these thoughtograph experiments serves to demonstrate the vast scope which exists and shows how easy it is to start experimenting yourself. Almost any inexpensive black and white film or printing paper can be used and they can be developed in an ordinary film tank or a couple of trays by the kitchen sink with perfectly safe chemicals that can be bought for a few coppers. A packet of the standard Kodak D76 developer, which makes a litre of developer enough to process ten 36-exposure 35 mm black and white films, only costs 61p, and a 250 ml bottle of Fix-Sol liquid fixer only costs 77p and, of course, if purchased in larger quantities works out even cheaper per film. Kodak or Polaroid instant print film packs, although more expensive, do give the great advantage of instant feedback of results which is always helpful in this sort of experiment.

Chapter 6

Beyond the spectrum

The range of electromagnetic radiation extends from the shortest of cosmic and X-rays to beyond the longest radio waves. Although we can only see the colourful spectrum of visible light, photographic emulsions are more sensitive and we can photograph further than we can see beyond both ends of the visible spectrum. This is one possible explanation for the appearance of the extra images on supernormal photographs.

Electromagnetic radiation travels like waves in water. The wavelength, that is the distance from the crest of one wave to the crest of the next, determines the colour of visible light and the intensity of the light is related to the height of the waves. These wave lengths range from the .000000001 mm of very short X-rays to the 10 million mm (10,000 m) of the longer radio waves which are measured in nanometres, one nanometre (an nm) being equal to one millionth of a millimetre. The very short waves are called X-rays when they are produced by an X-ray tube and gamma rays when they are given off by an atomic reaction, and overlap.

Our eyes can only see waves between about 400 nm (violet) and 700 nm (deep red) but bees can see ultra-violet light and some snakes detect their prey by its infra-red emissions. All photographic emulsions are, by their nature, sensitive to blue and ultra-violet light but can also be made sensitive to all wave lengths from the very shortest X-rays right through the ultra-violet and visible light and on into the infra-red, which has waves a little longer than the deepest red light that we can see.

X-ray photographs or radiographs are shadow photographs taken on special photographic emulsions made for this purpose, but ordinary photographic emulsions are also sensitive down to very short wave lengths. Extra images have appeared on X-rays of psychic people. X-ray photographs of Bertha Harris have contained some remarkable examples of this phenomenon and X-ray photographs taken of other people with psychic or paranormal talents have also, upon occasion, shown images which were not part of the normal photographic processes, but most of these seem to have been destroyed and information about them suppressed by the hospital departments concerned.

The high cost and danger involved in using the specialised equipment necessary prevents most of us from conducting further experiments with X-ray photography, although it would prove to be a fruitful field of study for a radiologist with an interest in the supernormal but both the ultra-violet and infra-red have been used for supernormal photography with varying degrees of success.

Photography is making pictures with light. Light passing through the lens of a camera forms an image on a light sensitive film. This image which is invisible is called a latent image and is made into a permanent visible image by developing the film. In black and white negative-positive photography this development involves several steps, each of which is simple but necessary. The latent image is formed by exposing the film in a camera, the film is developed to bring out a visible image, rinsed to check any further development, fixed by converting any unused sensitive chemicals into a soluble state, washed to remove the soluble residue and then dried. This provides us with a negative which must be printed by a similar process, usually on to a sheet of light-sensitive paper to obtain a positive picture. Coloured prints are made by a more complicated but basically similar process and transparencies are also made by a similar action of light on the negative material.

Most photographs are only produced when light created by or reflected from the subject is collected and directed by the camera lens so as to re-create an image of the subject of the photograph on the light-sensitive film. Supernormal photographs can be taken in just this way but many of them show extra images which were not visible when the photographs were taken. In these cases there are two possible hypotheses. Either they were made by some form of mental impression from the living photographic medium and are called thoughtographs or skotographs, or they are the images of deceased people and are psychic photographs.

Most photographic emulsions depend on the silver halides for their sensitivity to light. These halides are salts formed by the combination of silver with either bromine, chlorine or iodine, a group of elements which are called the halogens. The silver halides in photographic emulsions are sensitive to everything from the very shortest of X-rays to the deepest red light that we can see, but glass camera lenses absorb the radiations shorter than about 330 nm. Special lenses made of fluorite and quartz, instead of glass, are available for ultra-violet and infra-red photography.

The Rank Audio Visual Ltd Ultra-Achromatic-Takumar 85 mm f4.5 lens for ultra-violet photography at fairly close distances, which is made of fluorite and quartz and uses no glass at all and shows good results at all wave lengths from 220 nm to 1,000 nm, and the UA Takumar 300 mm f5.6 using glass and fluorite elements which is corrected for visible and infra-red light from 400 nm to 700 nm and is designed for telephotography in the visible and infra-red portion of the spectrum, can be used on any suitable 35 mm camera. The Zeiss UV-Sonnar 105

The electromagnetic spectrum

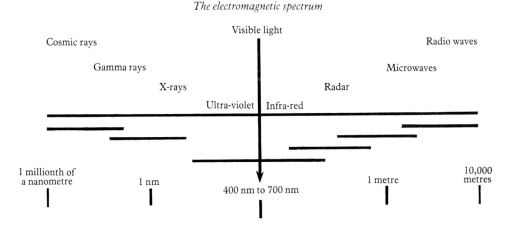

mm f4.3 lens, for use with the Hasselblad 500C and EL cameras, is made with quartz instead of glass and, although it is especially constructed to transmit ultra-violet radiation, it can also be used for photography in the visible spectrum as it has a wavelength range of from 215 to 700 nm. Rank Audio Visual Ltd tell me that their UA Takumars are priced at approximately £550 for the 300 mm and £750 for the 85 mm lenses and Hasselblad have informed me that their beautiful Zeiss UV-Sonnar is available to special order only and that its cost is in the region of £3,000.

For photographic purposes ultra-violet radiation is divided up into shorter and longer wave ultra-violet and, whilst the longer or near ultra-violet can be recorded without too much difficulty, fluorite lenses used in a vacuum with special film emulsions that are made with a very small amount of gelatin must be used to record very short far ultra-violet images, but such measures are too expensive and impracticable for most of us.

Special filters are available for ultra-violet and infra-red which can help us with our paranormal photography. Ultra-violet absorbing filters pass visible light but cut out ultra-violet radiation and can help to determine which part of the spectrum is making the extra images in supernormal photographs and, should it be the ultra-violet which is responsible, these extra images can then be enhanced by using an ultra-violet transmitting filter over the lens during subsequent exposures. This is a very dark glass filter which cuts out all visible radiation and only transmits the ultra-violet, so keeping any distracting visible images from affecting the film.

We have been discussing photography by reflected ultra-violet light but there is another way of using ultra-violet for supernormal photography. Some substances have the ability to absorb short wave radiation and then emit it at a longer wave length which is often part of the visible spectrum. This ability is called fluorescence if it stops almost immediately when the original exciting radiation is stopped and phosphorescence if it continues, as it sometimes does for hours, after the original radiation stops. It has been suggested that apparitions and ghosts have this ability to fluoresce and so become visible in a darkened room and, although such light emission is very dim, it can be photographed with ordinary films and cameras. Fluorescence and phosphorescence can be produced by almost any short wave radiation but ultra-violet light is usually used to excite them for photographic purposes. An ultra-violet absorbing filter must be placed in front of the camera lens so as to stop any direct ultra-violet radiation affecting the film and the ultra-violet light being used should be covered with a transmitting filter which only lets only it through and blocks off any other light. Such filters are readily available but the correct choice often depends on the type of lamp used to provide the ultra-violet light.

Ultra-violet fluorescent lamps, mercury lamps for producing a suntan, high pressure mercury arc lamps and even ordinary electronic photographic flash units can provide the ultra-violet illumination, but it should always be remembered that short wave radiation is dangerous. You should never be exposed to it for too long, eyes should always be protected from it by the correct type of ultra-violet goggles and even then you should never look directly at the lamp itself.

Opposite *Portrait of Commander Walter H. Lucas MBE of Southampton with spirit extras · taken by Mr Kanouse in Seattle, Washington, USA. In a letter dated May 3 1933, Lady Doyle commented favourably on the remarkable spirit photograph of her late husband Sir Arthur Conan Doyle (courtesy of Marcus Bray).*

William Henry Fox Talbot with one of his early cameras (courtesy of the Fox Talbot Museum).

The invisible infra-red waves are found just beyond the other end of the visible spectrum and anyone with a 35 mm camera and the necessary filters can take both black and white and coloured infra-red photographs. However, whilst most cameras are made of materials that are opaque to infra-red, some have plastic bodies or shutters that allow the infra-red through and, if you have one of these, you may get unwanted fogging or marking on the film. If you have any doubt about the infra-red proofing of your camera you can test it before using it for infra-red supernormal photography by loading it with an infra-red film and then moving a lighted 150-Watt lamp around the camera for a minute or two. If the film shows signs of fogging or marking after it is developed then the camera is not safe. Cameras can be proofed against infra-red by wrapping them in aluminium kitchen foil as a temporary expedient leaving a small opening around the lens and rangefinder windows where necessary, but it is better to work with an infra-red proof camera if possible.

Camera lenses are usually corrected so that the rays of all the different colours of the visible spectrum are focused on the same plane but, in most cases, the focus of the ultra-violet rays will be a little nearer to the lens and the infra-red image will be a little further from the lens than this focal plane. If the lens is well stopped down, both the near ultra-violet and the near infra-red will form an acceptable image. The infra-red image is actually formed about $\frac{1}{700}$ of the focal length of the lens behind the focal plane and many lenses cope with this by having a small red dot or a red letter R on the lens barrel to indicate the correct focusing position when you are using infra-red films. The method used is to first focus normally and then rotate the focusing barrel of the lens until the correct distance setting is moved in line with the red dot or R. The lens will now be focused for infra-red light.

If a flashgun is covered with an infra-red filter and used in the dark no filter is needed on the camera lens and only infra-red light will reach the film but, if you can see what you are photographing and only wish to record the infra-red light, then you need an infra-red filter on the lens.

Photoflood lamps also provide an excellent source of infra-red radiation but must also, of course, be covered by an infra-red filter for photography in the dark. Infra-red heat lamps are not suitable for photography as most of their radiation is in the far infra-red area and is well beyond the wave lengths to which infra-red film is sensitised.

Although infra-red films are more sensitive to heat than ordinary ones they can be safely kept at a temperature of about 13 degrees C (55 degrees F) for a few days but it is safer to store them in a refrigerator or freezer and they can be safely kept for months in a domestic freezer set at -18 degrees C (0 degrees F) or lower.

All infra-red film should be loaded in complete darkness and away from any heaters as infra-red radiation may leak in through the felt-lined slots of 35 mm cassettes and cause fog streaks to appear on the film. Exposure times given for infra-red films can only be used as a rough guide because so much depends on the filters and light sources used and it is advisable to bracket exposures by taking a series of three or five photographs at one or two stop intervals with the estimated exposure in the middle of the series.

Kodak Limited have made excellent information available in their booklet *Ultra-Violet Photography In Science and Industry Kodak Data Booklet SC-3* and in *An Introduction to Infrared Photography*, Kodak Information Sheet AM-900 (H), which can be obtained free of charge by sending a stamped and addressed large envelope to Kodak Limited, Product Services, PO Box 66, Station Road, Hemel Hempstead, Herts, HP1 1JU.

Kodak Ektachrome colour infra-red film is available in 20-exposure 35 mm cassettes and in boxes of 25 sheets of 4 × 5-inch cut film. Many specialist photographic dealers carry refrigerated stocks of these materials but they can be ordered for you by any dealer or camera shop and will then come fresh from Kodak.

Infra-red rays were discovered in 1800 by (Sir) William Herschel FRS, the celebrated astronomer, whilst he was investigating the solar spectrum and the ultra-violet rays that lay beyond the other end of the visible spectrum were discovered by J.W. Ritter in 1801 whilst carrying these investigations a stage further. In his book *The Pencil of Nature*, published in 1844, William Henry Fox Talbot, the inventor of the negative/positive process of photography, was the first to suggest the idea of taking a photograph in a completely dark room by using these invisible rays which lay beyond the spectrum.

The date of a supernormal photograph can often help us to determine the wave lengths of the radiation recorded in it. When the first psychic photographs were taken, in the days of wet plate photography, the active ingredient in the emulsions used were silver chloride, which is only sensitive to ultra-violet and violet light, and silver bromide, which extends the sensitivity to include blue light, and only these shorter wave lengths could be recorded. In 1873 H. Vogel in Germany discovered that a yellow dye used to prevent halation, the scattering of light inside the photographic emulsion, extended the sensitivity of the emulsion to the green part of the spectrum and by the early 1880s the dry plates, which had by then come into general use, were available with orthochromatic emulsions which included this new sensitivity to the green part of the spectrum.

Left *William Hope used an old Instantograph camera like this one to take spirit photographs (courtesy of the Kodak Museum).*

Below *John Myers took many successful psychic photographs using William Hope's old camera which he had acquired in 1930. This one, taken at the funeral of Lady Caillard in London, shows the spirit faces of Lord Caillard, Lady Caillard and Sir Arthur Conan Doyle.*

Right *Pictures of the past. This thermograph of a military airfield shows both aircraft that are still there and also, in the line-up on the extreme right, two aircraft that were there in the past but which have now flown away (courtesy of Hawker Siddeley Dynamics Ltd).*

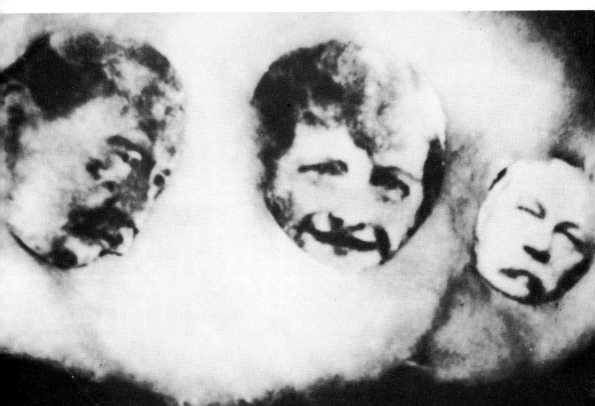

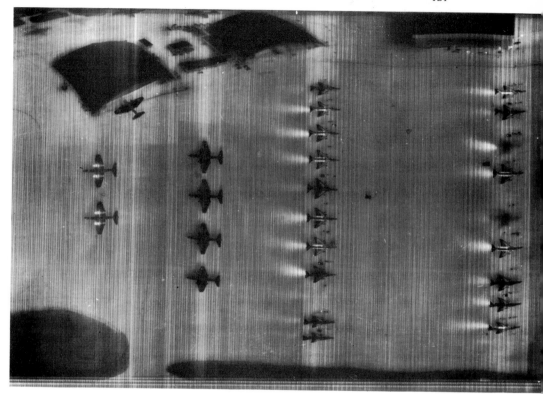

Panchromatic dyes which impart a sensitivity to the whole of the visible spectrum were introduced in Germany in 1904. These were not very sensitive to green light but modern panchromatic films are sensitive to all parts of the visible spectrum.

One novel attempt to extend the photographic spectrum used for recording paranormal phenomena was designed by Marcel Osty in April 1930. Marcel was assisting his father, Dr Eugene Osty, then the director of the *Institute Metapsychique* in Paris, France; in his investigation of Rudi Schneider, younger brother of Willi Schneider, who had been an outstanding physical medium since he discovered his abilities early in 1919 when he was 16 years old. Rudi first became aware of his talents in November of that year and the Schneider brothers were soon producing phenomena both at private seances and under laboratory conditions. As well as knocking and rapping noises there are many well authenticated cases of materialisations, levitations and the inexplicable moving of solid objects, all phenomena that we would describe today as examples of psychokinesis, occurring in their presence.

Dr Osty described the new equipment as an 'apparatus capable of registering photographically, automatically and at great speed, the phenomena produced by mediums in darkness'. In his 1932 F.W. Myers lecture 'Supernormal Aspects of Energy and Matter' given before the Society for Psychical Research Dr Osty said:

'As at that time plates sensitive to the infra-red were not yet available commercially, two categories of invisible radiations were made use of in order to attain the end we were aiming at. Infra-red rays were used to guard the object it was hoped to have displaced; ultra-violet rays were used for the photography.

Light on an invisible footprint. Taken with a pulsed laser this double exposure hologram is a 'ghost image' of the past; it shows the footprints on a piece of plain carpet of someone who had walked away from the chair ten minutes before the hologram was made (courtesy Dr W.R. Bradford).

'A projector of infra-red radiation directed a large beam of invisible light, reflected as often as required by a series of plane mirrors, at a photo-electric cell. The latter, by means of a relay, controlled the opening of a big shutter inserted in the ceiling of the seance room. As soon as any object entered into the infra-red beams this shutter opened rapidly and flooded the laboratory with ultra-violet light for $\frac{1}{10}$ of a second. Moreover, the opening of the shutter simultaneously produced the exposure of a camera provided with a quartz lens and taking a photograph of $\frac{1}{50}$ or $\frac{1}{100}$ of a second.'

Dr Osty and his son conducted 90 experiments with Rudi Schneider between October 1930 and the end of 1931. During the fourteenth of these, in November 1930, they used their new apparatus adapted to expose four cameras at the same time. Whilst Rudi was attempting to levitate a handkerchief protected by the infra-red rays of this apparatus, two sets of photographs were taken by the automatic devices as though the infra-red rays were being interrupted by something, but when the eight negatives were developed nothing unusual was seen on them.

This reinforces my own findings that paranormal phenomena react with the longer rays of the electro-magnetic spectrum rather than the shorter ones and is the reason for my preference for infra-red films for supernormal photography. With infra-red film in a conventional camera we can take photographs by its own radiation of anything heated to above 250 degrees C but special equipment is necessary if we wish to photograph anything cooler than that.

A new technique called thermography had to be evolved to photograph objects which were just warm rather than hot and the first successful thermographs of the human body were made by Dr Ray Lawson of Montreal in 1956. The special camera used for making thermographs today looks like a small television camera but is sensitive to infra-red rays instead of light. It produces black and white heat pictures on a display screen and, with the use of coloured filters, can produce a brilliant false colour display with the different false colours representing different temperatures. The display screen can then be photographed or videotaped to make a permanent record.

Amazingly thermographs can be used to make pictures of the past. Experimenters have made thermographs of an empty chair after the person sitting in it has gone away and the heat pattern left by the body shows up clearly and distinctly. We all leave these ghostly heat images behind us which can be recorded as thermographs and our past actions can now be traced through time. An emotional event or a traumatic experience may well leave some kind of image behind it in an analogous way and this is perhaps what we perceive when we see a ghostly apparition.

Living ghosts can also be produced by holography which re-creates a solid-seeming image of the original made only of light. A hologram is a recording or photograph that reproduces an image of the individual rays of light reflected from each point of an object's three-dimensional surface on a flat two-dimensional surface. It is made by splitting a beam of coherent light into two parts, one of which is bounced off the subject on to the emulsion of the film or plate whilst the other is simultaneously focused on to the same film. A light interference pattern is formed where the two beams overlap and it is this pattern that is recorded on the film. This interference pattern can be in the form of either a reflection hologram or a transmission holo-gram and when a similar beam of coherent light is reflected from the first or projected through the second type of hologram, a three-dimensional image is produced which is not flat like an ordinary stereoscopic photograph but is seen in the round so that you can look at it from different positions and see different aspects of it.

Holography was invented in 1947 by Professor Dennis Gabor, a Hungarian-born scientist working in Britain, and subsequently won him a Nobel Prize in Physics, but the first examples that he made using mercury vapour lamps as the light source were rather vague and unsharp.

The invention of the laser (light amplification by the stimulated emission of radiation) in 1958, and its later improvements the pulse ruby laser and the continuous wave gas laser, provided the beam of coherent light necessary for the further development of holography. Although light can be considered as a flow of either waves or particles the technique of holography depends on applying its wave aspect. As these waves of energy oscillate the wavelength determines the colour of the light and, when the wavelengths are all jumbled together like the wavecrests of a rough and stormy sea, all the colours are mixed together and white light is the result. This is called incoherent light. A laser produces light which is coherent with waves all the same length and oscillating in step with each other so that they rise and fall in perfect unison, when a hologram is re-created with a laser the images produced are optically indistinguishable from the real thing and are real in the same way that a ghost is real, but not solid. The large display of holograms of different kinds on show in the Light Fantastic Gallery in London's Covent Garden demonstrates many of these effects and shows how an apparently solid three dimensional object can in fact be a spectral image composed only of light.

One of the many wonderful phenomena associated with a holographic image is that all the information about the subject is simultaneously recorded on every point of the film so that you can cut the hologram up into little pieces and still reconstruct the image of the entire subject from any one small piece. For some time now the Home Office Police Scientific Development Branch have been working with EMI in developing a working method of picturing past events with new laser equipment that produces three-dimensional pictures of carpets which reveal the footprints of people who walked across them hours earlier, so helping the police to identify the criminals and time the crime.

Holographic images are more like the reported appearances of ghosts than anything else that we know and several research groups have suggested using holography to photograph ghosts and apparitions. One such group headed by Barry Taff, a parapsychologist, and Kerry Gaynor, a graduate of the University of California, Los Angeles, is associated with the Neuropsychiatric Institute of the University. With the aid of Dick Thompson, a professional photographer of Los Angeles, they have investigated and taken photographs of a number of haunted sites and houses in California and, on one occasion in 1976, recorded an extra image on photographs which was not visible in the room when the photographs were taken. On this occasion they were investigating a haunted house and several of the photographs showed an unusual arc of light near the woman who was the victim of the ghost's actions. They attended investigations at this house on seven different occasions as faint lights were seen when the room was darkened but only one dim image was recorded by using black and white film exposed with the light from an electronic flash unit covered with a deep red filter. It is interesting to note that this agrees with the findings of many researchers and mediums who find it easier to produce results in a room which is illuminated by only a dim red bulb.

Dick Thomson at first used Tri-X film in an ordinary single lens reflex camera with an automatic electronic flashgun fitted on top and the group gradually used more and more complicated equipment including high gain television cameras which work in very dim lighting. Theorising that, as a ghost is in many respects similar to a holographic image and that the ghostly image may well be produced by some analogous method, the Taff-Gaynor group's future plans include raising sufficient funds to obtain a holographic camera to use in their investigations and they go further still and will endeavour to capture a ghost by spraying it with liquid helium in an effort to solidify it and prevent it moving or fading away. The motion of molecules slows down as they get colder and when the temperature gets close to absolute zero all molecular movement ceases. Liquid helium is the coldest substance that we can handle and freezing a ghost with it may well help to show us how it is produced or, at very least, freeze it into place long enough to make a hologram of it.

Like this Taff-Gaynor group many scientific investigators often tend to use more complicated cameras and more esoteric equipment each time that they try to photograph the elusive extra images that appear on supernormal photographs only to find, as this group has found, that their only positive results are obtained when they use conventional cameras and equipment. The earliest photographic evidence of the supernormal was produced with the most elementary of cameras. The wet collodion plate cameras used were often just two wooden boxes, one sliding backwards and

Thermal imaging camera with power supply unit and pyrelectric vidicon (courtesy of English Electric Value Company Limited).

forwards into the other for focusing. The lens was of a simple two-element construction and, as was the practice at that time, the photographer prepared his wet plates himself immediately before using them. The longer exposures that were necessary in those early days were accompanied by development in trays until the image became visible, instead of the development in tanks by the time and temperature method used today. This itself may have been a factor in the success of the early psychic photographers.

If you have an old camera from the wet plate period or even an ordinary plate camera of the kind that our fathers and grandfathers owned, it can still be used today by going back to an even earlier photographic idea, the paper negatives which were invented by William Henry Fox Talbot the originator of modern photography. Instead of preparing our own sensitised paper today we can take a short cut and use ordinary glossy single weight printing paper, which works just as well and can be used for both the negative and the final positive print of your photograph. First a piece of cardboard is cut to fit into the slide holder of your camera. This will act as a template when you cut the printing paper in your darkroom or changing bag. When you have cut the paper to size, you can tape the two together to give the paper the additional thickness needed to hold it in place in the plate holders. After exposure the paper negative is developed in a tray. Inspection must be continued until the blacks are really black and any extra images are brought right out before using the stop bath and the fixer. If you do not have a proper darkroom with facilities to store chemicals you can buy small packets containing sufficient developer, stop bath and fixer for one session which are discarded after use and the same chemicals and paper can be used to make contact prints from the finished negatives.

Prints are made by wetting a fresh sheet of the paper in water, putting the negative with its emulsion side down on top of it so that the emulsions are in contact with each other and wiping with a sponge or squeegee to flatten them together and remove any surplus water. It should be exposed for about ten seconds, exact exposure instructions are packed with the paper, and processed in the same way as the negative. Using this simple process we can reproduce some of the conditions under which the early photographers of psychic phenomena worked and try to replicate their experiments.

Successful supernormal photographs have been taken with almost every kind of camera that has been made since the earliest days of photography, from the simple

Above *The arc of light seen over the victim of the haunting is one of the many effects recorded by Dick Thompson, a professional photographer from Los Angeles and a member of a group of researchers investigating a haunted house in Culver City (courtesy of Barry Taff).*

Left *The first Polaroid-Land camera, model No 95, circa 1948. Easily identified by the front sighting mast only made on this model.*

sliding box wet plate cameras and old Kodak box cameras right up to the newest Kodak Instamatics and Polaroid and Kodak Instant Print cameras and the most modern electronically controlled single lens reflex cameras. The sensitive film and plate emulsions used have been just as varied.

Kodak Ltd make a very large number of professional and specialist films in addition to the ordinary ones that are stocked by chemist shops and photographic dealers. Their Kodagraph Ghost Image Film G4, for instance, is a special film made for artists and draughtsmen which may well have interesting possibilities for supernormal photography. Available as either roll or sheet film, on a tough 'Estar' base which has a matt finish, it is designed for low intensity ghost images on to which data can be drafted. Kodak's extra fast Royal X Pan 120 roll film and Royal X Pan 4166 sheet film, which have a speed of ASA 1,250, and Kodak Recording Film 2475, a very high speed panchromatic 35 mm film which can be rated at ASA 4,000 and has an extended red sensitivity for available light photography, also have important implications for the photographing of supernormal phenomena which are so often inhibited by bright lights. Almost as useful in this respect is Ilford's new black and white HP5 which has a rated film speed of ASA 400 but which can be push-processed at least three stops higher so that it can be exposed at ASA 3,200. Pushing the film speed by extending the development time gives an additional bonus as it increases the negative contrast as well as increasing the effective speed of the film. This means that, in the conditions of low contrast and low level of incident light under which much supernormal photography takes place, the pushing of the film speed helps to give negatives that will print a full range of tones and help to show up details which might otherwise be lost. Kodak Ektachrome ASA 200 film for colour slides provides us with a colour material that can also be push-processed and still gives excellent results when exposed at ASA 1,200. For those who do not process their own film many commercial laboratories offer push processing as part of their service and these can be readily found in the advertising columns of photographic magazines. Your local photographic club can also put you in touch with enthusiastic amateur or semi-professional photographers who may be willing to process your films for you at a nominal cost and perhaps even become interested enough to join you in photographing the supernormal.

Kodak Ektachrome Duplicating film No 5071, more readily available in the USA than in Great Britain, has most interesting and exciting possibilities for supernormal photographic research as one of its basic attributes is a significant sensitivity to both ultra-violet and infra-red radiations beyond both ends of the spectrum of visible light. Although this film is designated as slide duplicating material, it can, of course, be used as ordinary photographic film in your camera and can be processed commercially or you can process it at home using the E6 process. It is a 35 mm slide film and has no edge markings, so it is even more essential than usual to keep careful notes of your subjects and exposure details for later identification if you use this film. Although it is not generally available from stock any dealer can order it from Kodak for you. It comes in 50-foot rolls which you have to rewind into standard cassettes, each roll providing enough film for approximately 13 standard 36-exposure cassettes.

Kodak also market several infra-red films which are of great importance in para-normal photography as, when they are used with a flashgun or photoflood lamp covered with an infra-red filter, you can take pictures in the dark. A further advantage is that, although the camera and film record the light that is reflected

Above *Miriam Daily with psychic extra. Miss Daily is now living in India and studying with Sai Baba the celebrated Indian mystic (courtesy of Catherine Andrews).*

Below *The No 1 Kodak camera of 1888—the camera which brought photography to the man in the street. The camera was loaded with 100-exposure film and, after exposing, camera, film and all were returned to the manufacturer for unloading and reloading. The loaded camera together with the camera case, cost £5-5-0d (courtesy of the Kodak Museum).*

from the scene before it, many subjects do not reflect the infra-red in the same proportions as the visible part of the spectrum and so by using infra-red film it is possible to record differentations that are not perceptible on ordinary film. These infra-red emulsions are especially sensitised to record the infra-red part of the spectrum but they are also just as sensitive to ultra-violet and blue light as other comparable photographic materials. When a photograph is taken with them an infra-red filter must be used over the lens, or over the light source if photographing solely by artificial light, as otherwise the result will be like an ordinary photograph.

For ordinary photography with black and white infra-red film a Kodak Wratten No 25 or 29 filter should be used, but for photography in the dark a No 87 or 88A filter, which will cut out all visible light, is necessary.

Kodak Ektachrome infra-red film is a false colour reversal film providing slides which are suitable for projection or reproduction. It differs from ordinary colour films in that the three emulsion layers are sensitive to green, red and infra-red instead of the usual blue, green and red. All three layers of colour infra-red films are sensitive to blue light so a yellow filter, such as the Kodak Wratten No 12 or 15 which are a deep yellow and cut out the blue light, should be used over the lens.

Kodak supply both the black and white and the colour infra-red films in 20-exposure 35 mm cassettes and the black and white film is also available in 4 × 5-inch sheets. They also make Kodak Aerochrome infra-red roll film 2443, but this is designed for aerial photography where it is often used for camouflage detection and in other specialised detection techniques. Infra-red films are very sensitive to heat and, wherever possible, should be stored in a refrigerator or, better still, in a freezer. Wrap the unopened packet of film in a sealed plastic bag before putting it in the refrigerator or freezer so that it does not get damp and take it out of the freezer so as to let the package defrost for three or four hours before using it.

Since George Eastman introduced the Kodak roll film camera in 1888 ever increasing numbers of photographers have been sending their films away for trade processing and the use of 35 mm film in still cameras, which commenced in 1913 with the production of the Homeos 35 mm stereo camera and which swept the world after the Leica 35 mm camera was produced in 1924, has meant that today the vast majority of amateur photographers and very many professionals send their exposed films away to be processed by specialised firms who use large automatic developing and printing machines. Thus the possibility that there has been fraud or cheating during the processing of supernormal photographs is now out of the question. This fool-proof photography is even more pronounced with the Polaroid Land system which yields a finished photograph on the spot. The Polaroid Land cameras first marketed in 1948 were not only a most important innovation in photography but were also a great step forward in the investigation of the supernormal. Another unintentional Polaroid benefit to supernormal photography is that the instant photographs produced by both the regular 'peel apart' Polaroid and the newer Polaroid and Kodak instant print cameras give the immediately available results which are so often an important factor in producing supernormal photographs.

Photographs produced with the first generation Polaroid cameras and films had a life expectancy of only about 10 or 12 years and it says much for the integrity of Dr Land and his process that large numbers of Polaroid pictures taken in those early days are still in perfect condition. But we are now 30 years on and, sadly, some of them are beginning to show signs of physical deterioration and fading which appears as patches of light or discoloured markings and can mislead the unwary.

Even though the newer Polaroid prints are much improved in quality and have greatly improved colour stability, as with any type of photograph exposure to light, particularly the ultra-violet wave lengths, will eventually cause them to fade and they can also be damaged by extremes of heat and humidity. Pulling the exposed Polaroid 'peel apart' film out of the camera through the squeegee rollers that break the pod of developing agent and spread its contents over the surface of the film, if done incorrectly, can produce defective prints with corners or patches of the picture missing or with striations and linear markings that are caused by dragging the exposed and coated film over a projection on the camera. Defective images can also be caused by allowing the photograph to develop for too long before peeling it from the negative or by developing it in too high or too low a temperature. Lines of fairly evenly spaced dots repeated across the picture are sometimes caused by dirt on the developer rollers and white or discoloured specks and larger markings can be made by pulling the picture out of the camera too quickly or too slowly. Variations of pressure or temperature over the area of the print during development may also affect the image and cause light or dark patches or incorrect colour casts to appear and all these must be very carefully guarded against when taking supernormal photographs. Physically produced markings such as these, which can appear on Polaroid photographs long after they are finished, are sometimes most misleading to investigators of paranormal phenomena and I have seen several supposed super-normal Polaroid pictures that were in fact caused in this way.

Although Kodak introduced their own colour instant print film pack and several new cameras in which it can be used, at the time of writing Polaroid is still the only supplier of instant black and white films. Polaroid no longer supply infra-red instant roll film but several of their current films have interesting implications for supernormal photography.

More than 25 different sizes and types of instant films are now available but, except for the 8 × 10-inch X-ray films, many of them are only the ordinary instant films in different packs or with different identification.

Polaroid instant black and white film Type 084, for instance, which is supplied for use by the medical profession, is the standard 3,000 speed 'peel apart' film Type 107, which we buy in 3¼ × 4¼-inch eight-exposure packs. Polaroid Type 664 3¼ × 4¼-inch pack film, which is designed for making cathode ray tube recordings, is a more interesting one for our purposes as, although its sharp cut off of highlights makes it unsuitable for ordinary photography, the long tonal scale which it gives in the dark areas of the photograph makes it a good film to use in the dim lighting conditions in which ghosts and apparitions are usually seen. Polaroid Type 410, an instant roll film yielding eight 3¼ × 4¼-inch pictures, has a speed of ASA 10,000 and, although this film is not generally available from dealers and would have to be specially ordered for you, it again gives really good results in very dim lighting conditions.

The light going through the lens in conventional cameras goes straight on to the film but in the Polaroid cameras which use SX70 Land instant film, the Kodak Instant cameras, the light which enters the lens is reflected by mirrors in the Polaroid cameras on to the front of the film and in the Kodak cameras on to the back, the opposite side of the image-forming surface. This, however, does not affect the use of these cameras for supernormal photography. I have seen several instant pictures of this type which have extra supernormal images on them and the

The Reverend Charles L. Tweedale and Mrs Tweedale with the spirit form of Mrs Tweedale's late father, Frank Burnett, who died in 1913. Photograph taken under test conditions by William Hope. In the photograph on the right of Frank Burnett, the only one showing him with a beard, he is wearing a hat.

people involved have found it most exciting to watch an extra image appear on a photograph just moments after they had taken the picture. Care is again needed in handling exposed films when they have been ejected from these cameras. They are both sensitive to heat and uneven temperatures whilst the picture is developing can cause blotches and clouding to appear. Polaroid SX70 Land film is also sensitive to pressure whilst it is developing and for some time afterwards and, whilst the Mylar cover of the SX70 print is very tough, pressing on it or bending it bruises the image underneath and causes coloured shading and markings which should not be misinterpreted as extra images. If a Polaroid SX70 Land camera is held with a finger or fingers blocking the picture exit slot under the front edge of the camera, horizontal creases and varicoloured markings, yellowish blotches, feathery white blemishes or a combination of all or any of these may show on the finished photographs and similar markings may result if the photograph is bent or creased sharply. A finger pressing against the bellows of the camera can cause photographs to be fogged, to have cloudy or streaky light patterns or, if the action of the mirror is stopped, even to be completely white, whilst a finger in front of the flash bar can possibly reflect some of the light back into the lens thus fogging the picture and a finger in front of the lens can cause a blur or dark mark on the photograph.

The fine satin pebble grained surface of the Kodak instant print film is less liable to show pressure marks, but the rear of the film unit is not so resistant and any undue pressure on it will mark the print. These possibly misleading defects which occasionally mar an instant photograph are not given as a reason for not using these cameras but as a precautionary warning to experimenters on the meticulous care needed when these films and cameras are used for supernormal photography.

All scientific research must be conducted with great care and when investigating supernormal photography we must constantly guard against the introduction of photographic defects which, in this case, might be misinterpreted as supernormal extra images. All photographic manuals emphasise the necessity of careful and clean processing and this is doubly necessary for those involved with supernormal photography. Because of the elaborate precautions and extensive testing continuously used by manufacturers and the better processors, the chance of defects caused by faulty materials or processing is so small that it assumes negligible proportions and, for this reason, I now have all my supernormal photographs processed by a reputable commercial organisation. This allays any fear that I might have deliberately or inadvertently tampered with the images.

Home processing needs even more than the usual care. All water and solutions should be carefully filtered as rust or corrosion of pipes or particles of undissolved developer can damage the film and even a puff of powdered developer which sometimes spreads in the air when it is weighed out carelessly can cause unforeseen trouble.

Patchy aerial fog, caused when the film is developed with insufficient agitation near the surface layer of the developer which is rich in dissolved oxygen, and dichroic fog which can be formed by transferring the film directly from the developer to a neutral hypo bath without an intermediate rinse or stop bath, can both cause disconcerting extra cloud-like images on the film and should be carefully guarded against. Many other possible processing defects can affect the image on the finished film. If the film is not agitated properly in the developer, light bromide streamers sometimes flow from the dark areas and dark developer streamers may come from the light areas of the negative. Fogging and veiling of part of the image is

The Contax RTS II Quartz body fitted with Data Back Quartz D-4 is one of a number of cameras which imprint information directly on to the negative when the picture is taken.

sometimes seen. If the markings or fogging covers the edges of the film it was probably caused by light acting before or after the photograph was taken or by chemicals during processing, but if the edges of the film are not fogged then the markings were caused in the camera. Fogging is sometimes caused in the camera by light leaking through a small pinhole or around a loose-fitting camera back. This fogging usually shows as a band or streak and its position may give a clue to the point from which the light leak came. If the camera is free from any light leaks the image probably has a supernormal cause. Patches of lighter density on negatives which show as dark areas on the print may be caused by uneven immersion in the hypo fixing bath or the developer, and fixer splashed on to the film before it is developed will also cause clear or nearly clear patches on the negative. Finger-print markings can be easily identified but if the finger tips are wet, very greasy or contaminated with chemicals and the film is touched before development, small round or oval light patches are formed. Larger light or blank patches can also be caused by two parts of the film touching each other whilst being developed, thus preventing the solution from reaching them. Tangled ribbon trails and markings looking like a child's scribble sometimes cover the negative. This occurs when a camera with a pin hole in its bellows, body or between the lens shutter is carried about in the bright sunshine. The pin hole can form an image of the sun on the film and, as it is moved about, a continuous scribbled line is drawn on the emulsion. In diffused light such a pin hole can cause small dark patches, fading towards the edges, to appear on the film. This defect does not occur in modern cameras with focal plane shutters which cover the film when it is not being exposed as a pinhole in the blind of a focal plain shutter just causes a slightly denser line in the negative.

Mottled markings on negatives are sometimes caused by using old developer or old film and occasionally by leaving the film exposed to the air in the camera for periods of many months or more, and the simple answer to this is always to use fresh materials and to process them promptly after exposure. Uneven dark streaks on a negative and the corresponding light streaks on a print are sometimes caused by dirty dishes and undefined clear areas, at one side or in one corner of the negative, can be caused by a finger or part of the camera case partly covering the lens. Two images on the same negative can, of course, be caused by double exposure, but this is not possible with most modern cameras unless the film is deliberately rewound and then wound on again, a process which can more often than not be detected by the overlapping frame edges showing in the negative. Mottling or patches of light can also be formed on prints which are not kept moving about in the developer, fixer or washing, or which are inadvertently splashed with chemicals. But again care and cleanliness in processing is the answer.

In most cases there is no difficulty in differentiating between extra images which are produced supernormally and those caused by the aberrations or defects that the normal photographic processes are sometimes subject to. A small percentage of the photographs which have been submitted to the Bureau for the Investigation of Paranormal Photographs have shown markings which an experienced photographer can recognise as having a normal physical origin.

The traditional photographic materials have there own different types of defects which produce different markings, including the lightning-like streaks and flares on 35 mm and roll film negatives which can be caused by static electricity. These effects, although rare, are more prevalent when the air is very dry and in such conditions it is sensible to rewind film—especially 35 mm—much more slowly than usual. Bar or moisture static is a less well known condition which can cause a general fogging of the film in a bar-like pattern, usually with a localised variation of density in the bar pattern, sometimes in the shape of spots which generally result from a discharge of static electricity in moist conditions. Static charges can be produced by the friction of layers of film slipping over each other, by film rubbing against edge guides, rollers or pressure backs in cameras, or by the close layers of film being pulled apart. Static marks on black and white negative film are black and show as white marks on the prints and on colour films they are usually coloured, the colour depending on which layers of the film have been affected.

Extra images sometimes appear on finished prints, although the negatives themselves may show no trace of them. Investigation has borne out the authenticity of most of those that I have examined but here, too, one must be especially careful of modern materials. On some of the newer resin-coated printing papers, for instance, which in the main give a poor quality black, a very deep black sometimes leads to deposits of silver on the surface of the emulsion which look like patches of fog or print deterioration and can be misinterpreted. These photographic defects are very uncommon but they must all be carefully considered in conjunction with the type of material, processing and camera used and any other confirmatory evidence available when vetting supernormal photographs.

One photographer has even reported that he had inexplicable fogging and marks on the negatives taken with his Hasselblad camera. Whilst it is unlikely that a camera of this quality would have a fault, the camera was checked thoroughly until he was convinced that there was nothing wrong with it. He was baffled for months until a chance suggestion from a friend pinpointed the answer to the problem. The photographer had been keeping his spare films in the same cupboard as some luminous compasses and the radiation from the compass dials had fogged the films in the same way that X-rays do. This emphasises the need for the background investigation which should always accompany any investigation of supernormal photographs. There are, at the moment, so many unknown variables involved in the taking of supernormal photographs that we are forced to use what artists call 'in-process discovery'. A painter, for instance, does not visualise the entire finished picture when he sits down before a blank canvas, any more than a poet sees his entire poem or a writer his entire book. The picture often seems to grow on the canvas under its own volition. This mystery of creativity seems to extend to the process of producing supernormal photographs. The multiple reactions between the photographer, medium, environment and the photographic processes them-selves makes it necessary for us to involve ourselves in a many-voiced discussion and to be willing to try any and every alternative methods that is available to us to capture the elusive extra images. It is essential, however, to do this in an orderly manner and to keep adequate if not comprehensive notes.

The basic data of camera and lens, lighting, film, aperture and shutter speed can be self recorded by the camera if one with a data back such as the Asahi Pentax K2DMD or the Canon AEI is used, but can easily be noted on a tape-recorder or in the journal of experiments which should always be kept up to date. The Canon AEI, or any other camera with a similar electronic self-timer and an auto winder or motor drive, can be used on a tripod or stand to take time lapse photographs so as to monitor a haunted place for a short time automatically. If you set the self-timer, screw in a cable release and lock it and press the shutter, the auto-winder will take a series of 36 exposures at ten-second intervals over a period of six minutes, setting you free to use a ciné camera or another still camera loaded with film which has a different sensitivity range at the same time.

The journal of experiments and notes which should be kept by any scientific investigator should be written up preferably during but, at the very least, immediately after each session and checked and witnessed by all present in order to prevent any lapse or failure of human memory affecting your conclusions or results. Remember to include the names and addresses of everyone present and, if you are taking Kodak or Polaroid instant photographs, to have these signed, dated and authenticated immediately by everyone concerned.

Equally important but sometimes less obvious is the recording of such variables as the time of day, maximum and minimum temepratures and even the compass setting and the atmospheric humidity and pressure. These will aid in the replication of successful experiments and will help to screen out artifacts such as the bars and streaks of light that sometimes appear as the result of camera movement in flash-light photographs taken in poor lighting conditions when the flash freezes the action of the central foreground images but bright background lights are recorded as blurred or moving blobs of light because of camera shake.

Spectacular films of the supernormal have been made with ciné cameras and psychics and seances have been the subjects of many extraordinary motion pictures. Recent films of the supernormal have included a two-hour long documentary *A Journey into the Beyond* which opens with a commentary by Ed Mitchell, the astro-naught who conducted a successful telepathy experiment from space to Earth during his flight to the moon. This shows authentic examples of psychic healing, materialisation and many other supernormal phenomena. In one scene, filmed during a seance in the Roman catacombs, ectoplasm flowing from the mouth and nose of an Italian medium can be seen building up into a larger than life figure

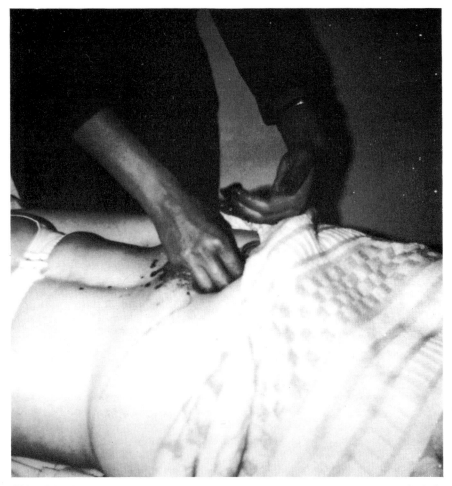

Helen Elizalde operating on Mrs Harrison of Huntingdon. The medium holds a large blood clot between the fingers of her left hand. Mrs Harrison was suffering from back pain. After the operation the pain had gone (courtesy of Brian Hurst).

which advances with arms outstretched and then dissolves away. Another scene in this film shows a red-robed African standing in a ring of fire slowly and with great effort of will 'levitating until he is floating in mid-air, descending and rising again before finally collapsing on the ground'.

The feats of the ubiquitous Uri Geller have, of course, been filmed and videotaped many times. In 1973 the Stanford Research Institute produced a film of a series of tests conducted with him in November and December 1972, *Experiments with Uri Geller*, which can be hired from Ed Mitchell's Institute of Neotic Sciences by universities and scientific research organisations. The film shows five tests one each for telepathy and clairvoyance, two for psychokinesis, and one in which Geller influenced the reading of a Bell magnetometer by moving his hands around it causing an 0.3 gauss deflection of the meter. In addition there are two further tests which were not considered positive enough to be entirely satisfactory in which Geller apparently moves a compass needle and bends a stainless steel spoon by supernormal means. Although subsequent research has suggested tighter experimental controls and techniques, this film is still a good example of the value of motion pictures in investigating the supernormal.

Another documentary film, *A Study of a Psychic*, made in Canada by The Bruce Raymond Film Company of Toronto, Canada, deals with the psychic powers of Mathew Manning, whose strange supernormal talents first became apparent when as an 11-year-old schoolboy, he was involved in an outbreak of poltergeist activity in his home. Although this faded away after a few weeks the violent activity started up again four years later and followed Mathew to his boarding school. This poltergeist activity died away as his supernormal talents developed and, as he grew up, he discovered that he could read minds, bend metal and, on occasion, foretell the future. He has also developed a talent for producing psychic drawings and automatic writing.

Although the resources of a professional film crew give them a great advantage, anyone with a ciné camera can take supernormal motion pictures and, in many cases, can produce first class evidential films simply by being in the right place at the right time. One such opportunity was taken by Shirley and Carl Lehman during their first visit to the Philippines in 1972. A psychic surgeon removed a cyst which had been growing on Carl's foot for 20 years. But he and Shirley managed to watch psychic surgeons operating on many patients and they took 600 ft of coloured film and over a hundred slides, including many close-ups of the spirit operations.

Michael Bingham, another dedicated investigator of supernormal phenomena, has made several flights half-way around the world from his home in New Zealand to track down the ghosts of Chingle Hall at Goosnargh near Preston, one of Britain's most famous haunted houses. Armed with ciné and still cameras and a tape-recorder, Michael has discovered two secret compartments in the solid-seeming walls which appear to have been used to hide priests during the persecutions of the Catholics in the 16th century. On his last trip to England, in February 1977, Michael called to see me and showed me an 8 mm film that he had taken during one of his nightly vigils at Chingle Hall. Only the last 20 ft of the film were significant. In this sequence one can see a ghostly shape moving along the hallway on the first floor of Chingle Hall going towards the far end, pausing in the doorway there and then retracing its steps. The film unfortunately ran out after the ghost had taken three or four steps back towards the camera. The film is very dark. The camera was placed on a tripod at the end of the hall about 30 ft away from the doorway and the only light was from an unshielded 100-Watt bulb hanging below the camera. Michael was in a room off the hall to the left of the camera and exposed the film by remote control when he heard the footsteps. These phantom footsteps started a few feet in front of, and to the left of, the camera, walked towards the doorway at the far end of the hall, halted and walked three or four steps back towards the camera before stopping, corresponding exactly to the actions of the shape that is seen on the film. One frame in this strip is of great interest because it is partly illuminated by an ectoplasmic drapery or curtain which appears in the room at the far end of the hall and is clearly visible through the doorway obstructing almost half of the large window on the other side of the room.

Almost any ciné camera and film can be used for supernormal photography but the latest XL super 8 cameras, with very fast lenses and extra large shutter sector

Poltergeist activity photographed at Air Heating, Leeds (courtesy of Andrew Green).

openings used with the new faster films that are now available, are designed especially for use in the dim light in which much supernormal photography takes place.

Polaroid's instant motion picture film and equipment have the same advantage over conventional ciné cameras that their still instant photographs have over the ordinary photographic processes when used for supernormal photography. Their production of the instant feed-back of results is so exciting and encouraging to the researcher and so conducive to further positive results. To make a Polaroid instant movie all you have to do is to drop a cassette of film into the camera, aim and shoot. After you have taken your moving pictures you take the film cassette out of the camera and place it in a slot in the top of the player. In about 90 seconds the moving pictures have been processed in the cassette and appear on the player's 12-inch screen, allowing you to record supernormal phenomena and achieve almost instant playback. The film used in the Polaroid instant cassette is magnetically sound striped super 8 so the provision of direct sound recording cameras was probably envisaged from the start and this again adds an extra dimension to the possibilities of this system for supernormal motion picture photography.

Almost since the first public presentation of the *Lumière Cinématographe* moving pictures in Paris in 1895, ciné cameras have been used to record scientific and supernormal experiments and phenomena of all kinds and, although portable video-tape cameras and recorders offer similar results, the cost and bulk of such units make them impracticable for most of us at present.

Parapsychologists and professional investigators of the supernormal usually come complete with cameras, tape-recorders and an amplitude of apparatus but it would be wonderful if we were all more prepared to meet the supernormal when it surfaces in our everyday lives and were ready to make a photographic record of the events which occur. What usually happens is that the very unexpectedness of the phenomena catches everyone involved by surprise and it is often all over before even a note can be made of what is happening. Few of us, even in these camera-conscious times, keep a loaded camera handy and so good photographs of spontaneous supernormal phenomena are rare. Despite this, however, we do have an amazing fund of authentic photographs that show supernormal extra images, many of them taken by people who were completely unaware of their psychic talents.

Chapter 7

What are supernormal photographs?

The key question in our enquiry is, of course, 'what are supernormal photographs?' Many manufacturers of photographic materials and commercial processing firms have from time to time given me different explanations of this amazing phenomenon. One suggested that the film or paper on which the extra image was recorded had been stored next to a photograph or picture which had somehow filtered through the black wrapping! A manufacturer of films said that the extra images were caused by faulty processing and processing organisations suggested that they were being caused by faulty films but, as each denied that they were responsible and proved this to my satisfaction, it became obvious that many of these anomalies of the photographic process could only have a supernormal origin.

Many investigators have made the mistake of lumping all supernormal photographs together. There are several different types of supernormal photographs, several different causes which influence the photographic emulsion and there are a number of different ways in which supernormal photographs can be produced. To deny that supernormal photographs exist or can be produced, as some people have done because their existence does not seem to be compatible with some of our accepted scientific ideas, is also a mistake. The evidence of supernormal photographs is real but the emotional content of the subject has caused it to be denied the logical approach and investigation to which it is entitled.

Although many of the extra images seem at first glance to appear at random, careful investigation shows that there must be some reason or intelligence behind them. Spiritualist mediums have been amongst the leaders in this field and many have told me that there is no doubt in their minds that their supernormal photographs are created by the discarnate intelligence of the deceased but this, however well evidenced, is only one of the number of possible theories which have been put forward.

Sensible, stable citizens, in no way connected with Spiritualist circles, have produced supernormal photographs and on some photographs the extra images have appeared apparently of their own volition. In other cases people entirely uninterested in psychic matters have unwillingly and unwittingly produced supernormal photographs of great interest. There seems to be no doubt that some unknown knack or talent is required to produce these extra images on photographs and it would seem that this talent is not confined to a few people but, like dowsing, is latent in many of us.

The amount of energy needed to affect the sensitive photographic emulsion is

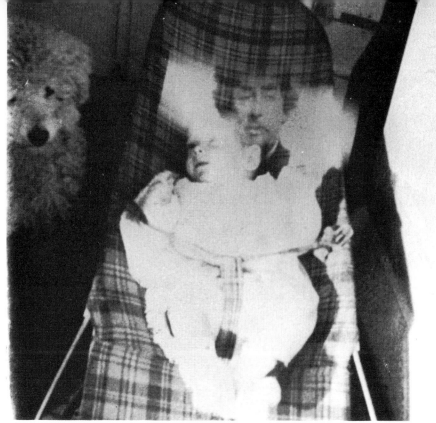

'I have never seen anyone resembling the dark stranger with the disdainful look,' said Mrs Edwina Postelthwaite when the man's face appeared on the Polaroid photographs that she took of her baby Lynn (courtesy of Dennis Johnstone).

very small and is of the order that can be emitted by the human body. This lends support to the theory that some form of human bio-energy is involved and, if this is so, then its control by the conscious or sub-conscious mind would be an acceptable suggestion. The mental influence on physical matter demonstrated by powers such as levitation and psychokinesis is now well accepted and this may indeed be the way that supernormal photographs are produced.

When evaluating supernormal photography people will often suggest that fraud or trickery of one sort or another is involved but to suggest that, for instance, William Hope practised such fraud continuously whilst producing supernormal photographs under strict conditions for nearly 30 years really shows the absurdity of the suggestion.

Paranormal and psychic experiments have been plagued by this possibility of fraud. Modern Spiritualism started with the activities of the Fox sisters in the United States and, as soon as they started making money from their mediumistic talents, many other mediums jumped on to the bandwagon. Although many of these professional mediums had some real powers and produced traces of genuine phenomena, these were soon admixed with fraudulent practices made necessary by the pressure of regular public performances on the mediums' sometimes meagre talents.

The parlour tricks which were sometimes played upon our Victorian ancestors have, however, no place in modern parapsychological and psychic research and fraudulent mediums are unmasked as soon as they leave the small circle of their

Above *Spirit photograph taken with the deep trance healer as the graphic medium. Exposure $\frac{1}{25}$ second at f11 in a dimly lit room.*

Left *J.H. Evans with the spirit of Kate Owen. Photograph by Boursnell 1895.*

Above right *Ectoplasm can be seen coming out of the front of the medium's neck in this infra-red photograph of one of Jack Webber's seances. A burst of light or energy is often seen in photographs of materialisations although, as in this case, it is usually not visible at the time (courtesy of Ray Branch).*

immediate credulous clients. With the use of infra-red films and light-intensifiers the activities which go on in even a completely darkened seance room are as easily seen as if they were taking place in broad daylight. Monitoring with cine cameras or videotape recorders will uncover the most dexterous sleight of hand or conjuring that might be tried.

My experiments with supernormal photography have, in the main, been carried out with non-professional psychics and, when I have conducted research with professional healers, mediums and psychically-talented people, we have always agreed that there must be no financial consideration involved. I must express my thanks to the many professional clairvoyants, healers and mediums who have freely donated their valuable time and talents to help me in this work.

Even photographic evidence of the supernormal on its own is only valuable if the details of the circumstances under which the photographs were produced are known and this again is another reason for conducting your own research so that you will be able to control events yourself.

The story of the pioneer of electricity, Ampère, is often given as an explanation of the need for a push to start off some kinds of phenomena. Giving a new demonstration of electricity before a scientific committee, a galvanometer needle failed to move at the critical moment and Ampère gave it a touch with his finger. Repeating the experiment, successfully this time, he pointed to the needle and said triumphantly, 'This time it goes of itself!' Psychic phenomena are no exception to this but the push that is needed is, unlike Ampère's, a non-physical one and consists mainly of a positive attitude on the part of the researcher, psychic and all present to the experiment.

Left *The white kitten being held by this little boy was killed by a St Bernard dog soon after Major Wilmot Allistone took this photograph in Clarens, Switzerland.*

Below *This photograph was taken by Major Allistone in August 1925. Several weeks after the kitten died the boy is seen holding a toy rabbit and an extra miniature image of the cat's head can be seen above the empty right hand.*

If the medium is able to produce a materialisation it is especially desirable to photograph the medium and the extra image together on the same negative. The appearance of such materialisations which are often only nebulous and partially-formed clouds, out of which the appearance slowly solidifies, is unpredictable and sometimes one must wait for hours before the first indications appear. It is difficult to keep up constant alertness under these conditions and this is another reason for having cameras and equipment constantly ready so that as soon as something does seem to be happening it can be instantly recorded.

In some cases materialisations seem to rise up through the floor. Professor Richet reported that during his experiments in 1904 he saw: 'A fully organised form rise from the floor. At first it was only a white opaque spot about the size of a handkerchief lying on the ground before the curtain, then this handkerchief quickly assumed the form of a human head, level with the floor, and a few moments later it rose up in a straight line and became a small man enveloped in a kind of white burnous, who took two or three halting steps in front of the curtain and then sank to the floor and disappeared as if through a trap door. But there was no trap door!'

Many other observers have also told of similar materialisations and dematerialisations and of what seemed to be living hands melting away and disappearing whilst being clasped in the hands of the researcher. Amongst the best known photographs taken of these materialisations are those of Bien Boa and Katie King. Another famous series is the seven sequential infra-red photographs of the materialisation of Silver Belle, spirit guide of the famous medium Ethel Post-Parish, which were taken over a period of about 20 minutes and show a cloud of ectoplasm gradually building up and solidifying into the fully formed figure of the Indian girl whilst witnesses sat on the floor less than two feet away.

Researchers have reported and photographed many different kinds of materialisations. With some mediums a kind of liquid or pasty jelly emerges from the mouth, forehead or breast, with others thin, narrow stalks which thicken, little by little, into muslin-like curtains or even solid-seeming limbs and bodies are extruded. Materialisations usually take place gradually, changing from rudimentary masses and shapes to complete forms and faces. They are often at first very imperfect. Sometimes they show no relief, looking almost like flat two-dimensional cut outs rather than solid bodies.

The fact that some materialisations appear to be flat images rather than three-dimensional solid forms should not be taken as evidence of trickery or fraud. There is no reason to assume that materialisations must have depth and be three-dimensional like a human body. The moist, gelatinous and semi-luminous extensions that came out of the mouth and body of Eva C, for instance, were embryonic formations which tended towards organisation and image without immediately achieving it. Many of the faces seen in the materialisations of Eva C were flat and two-dimensional rather than three-dimensional figures, often looking like drawings that have been creased or folded and straightened out again.

These flat images appeared in cases when her hands were never out of sight and the extreme vigour of the conditions and the minute inspection of her person both before and after her seances made it impossible for her to have hidden large drawings. They appeared outside the veil of tulle that covered her and there were very evident life-like movements in these images which rapidly succeeded one another and seemed to be living things.

Her experiments with Dr Schrenck-Notzing and Madame Bisson, which lasted

Above *The plate and camera for this psychic photograph by William Hope were provided by S. De Brath.*

Left *This photograph of Mrs Lillian Cipin and Mrs Sadie Permutt shows a burst of psychic energy.*

Above right *Spirit photograph by William Hope certified by S. DeBrath, an experienced psychic researcher.*

Right *'This was taken while we were in the circle listening to the organ music. You can see the organist at the back of the photo, my spectacles can be seen just behind him, then me. The glow of light is where the medium sits, she is blotted out with a round light of power. Then power is visible by the rays you see from the top corner. Another unit of power is beginning to build up at the bottom. The camera is just left exposed. No one touches it or goes near it so our friends must manipulate for us to get these results.'* *(Mrs H. Kelly.)*

Dr. G. Geley →   ← S. DeBra...

I certify that this photograph was taken at Crewe by W^m
Hope, Nov. 1919, on plates bought in London same day, opened by me and signed, not lost sight of during the whol
process. Recognised by the lady's brother (non-spiritualist)
and by three intimate friends. She "died" Aug. 1913. There
is no similar portrait extant.   S. De Brath. M.Inst.C.E.

over four years, were conducted with admirable care and patience and minute precautions were taken against fraud. At each seance the cabinet, which was just a corner of the room cut off by a curtain, was closely searched. Eva was completely undressed and, in the presence of the experimenters, clothed in a close fitting garment covering her from head to foot. Her head was covered by a veil of tulle sewn to the other garment. Her hair, armpits, nose, mouth and knees were examined and in some cases even examination *per rectum et vaginam* was resorted to in order totally to ensure that nothing was concealed about her person.

As the materialised substance frequently came from her mouth, syrup of bilberries (whose deep colouring powers are well known) was administered but, notwithstanding this, the extruded forms were absolutely white. Experimental rigour was even pushed to the point of giving her an emetic before the seance.

The light in front of the curtain was sufficient to allow large print to be read. Behind the curtain was a red and a white light which could be put on at will. At least three cameras, including a stereoscopic one, were focused on the cabinet ready to be worked at a signal and sometimes as many as nine were used.

Eva, having been undressed in full light and clothed as described above, was brought into the cabinet, the curtains were drawn, the light reduced and the experiments began. Under these circumstances it seems physcially impossible that any fraud could occur. There was no way that an accomplice could enter or any way that Eva might bring any objects with her. Moreover, Eva lived with Madame Bisson who rarely left her. The two ladies took their meals together and slept in the same room.

It is not possible that Dr Schrenck-Notzing, Dr Geley, J. Maxwell, Dr Bourbon, M. Chevreul, C. de Vesme, G. de Fontenenay, Professor Richet and the many other scientists, doctors and psychical researchers who assisted at and supervised at experiments conducted at Algiers, Biarritz, Munich and Paris, which extended over four years, could all have been so extensively deceived if there had been any doubt as to the authenticity of the materialisations that she produced.

These seemed to consist of a luminous and mouldable emanation from her mouth, navel and when she was completely nude, alone with Madame Bisson, sometimes from her breasts and armpits. It is a whitish substance that creeps as if alive with damp, cold protoplasmic extentions which are transformed under the eyes of the experimenters into a hand, fingers, a head, or even into an entire figure.

Similar almost two-dimensional effects are seen in many of the materialisations produced during the research conducted by Dr T. Glen Hamilton (with Mrs Mary Marshall as the medium) from 1928 until his death in 1935. Dr Hamilton made photographic records of these materialisations, many of which are shown in his book, *Intention and Survival*, Regency Press, London, 1977, and in *Is Survival a Fact?* by his daughter Margaret Lillian Hamilton, BA, Psychic Press Ltd, 1969. He often used groups of cameras, including stereoscopic cameras and cameras with quartz and wide angle lenses, and differing photographic emulsions to record the phenomena so as to make his work as comprehensive as possible. He obtained more than 300 exposures of 52 separate materialisations.

Dr J.W. Crawford of Belfast made a similar extensive photographic record of the materialisations produced by Kathleen Goligher, another non-professional medium. Some of his photographs are shown in his book, *The Psychic Structures at the Goligher Circle*, and a number of these have a similar flat, two-dimensional appearance.

Taken from a sequence of seven infra-red photographs depicting the whole process of materialisation of a spirit form. Taken in about 20 minutes. An assistant holds the curtain to reveal the entranced medium, Ethel Post-Parrish. A cloudy pillar of ectoplasm slowly builds from the medium to the height of a full-grown woman. Gradually the ectoplasm solidifies until finally the full figure emerges, completely materialised. It is Silver Belle, an Indian girl said to be the medium's spirit guide. 81 people were present, including a number of sceptics. None found fault with the test conditions, or the results. Ralph Pressing, *editor of* Psychic Observer, *sat on the floor less than 2 ft away (courtesy of* Psychic News*).*

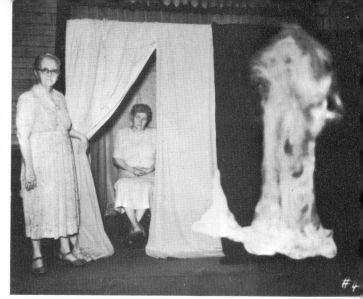

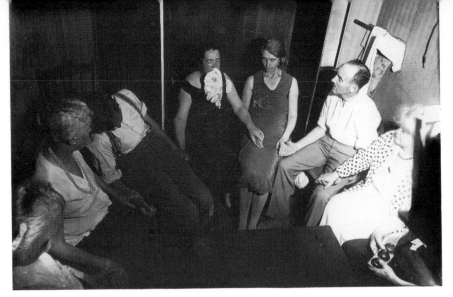

The archives of the Bureau for Investigation of Paranormal Photographs contain a considerable number of the original photographs produced by Doctors Hamilton and Crawford, many of which were kindly sent to me by Dr Hamilton's daughter, Margaret Lillian Hamilton, and the two-dimensional effect can be clearly seen, especially on those taken with stereoscopic cameras.

A recent *Daily Telegraph* mention of a haunted house in Bath interestingly supports the actuality of this two-dimensional appearance by reporting that the ghosts which are often seen by visitors to the house always show themselves as two-dimensional profile images.

Supernormal and psychic photography is the subject of this book because, although investigators have tried many different methods and used many different instruments and machines in their endeavours to record psychic phenomena, photography has been the only one which has consistently produced successful results.

During the American Civil War, the seances held by President Abraham Lincoln in the White House gave a boost to Spiritualists and led many of them to try to build instruments which would amplify or record the forces that caused materialisations and moved furniture in their seance rooms. Professor Robert Hare, MD, was an early pioneer of this work and in *Experimental Investigation of Spirit Manifestations*, first published in 1855, he described and illustrated several pieces of apparatus which he had devised and used to prove the existence of supernormal forces and phenomena. Many different versions of the planchette and other simple devices were available for experimenters but little real progress was made until technical developments, forced up in the hot house of two world wars, led to a resurgence of interest in such instrumentation.

In the October 30 1920 issue of *Scientific American*, Thomas Alva Edison, the technical wizard and one of the world's greatest inventive minds who sincerely believed in survival, said; 'If our personality survives then it is strictly logical and scientific to assume that it retains memory, intellect and other faculties and knowledge that we acquire on this earth. Therefore if personality exists after what we call "death", it is reasonable to conclude that those who leave this earth would like to communicate with those they have left here . . . I am inclined to believe that our personality hereafter will be able to affect matter. If this reasoning is correct, and if we can evolve an instrument so delicate as to be affected, or moved, or manipulated by our personality as it survives in the next life, such an instrument, when made available, ought to record something.'

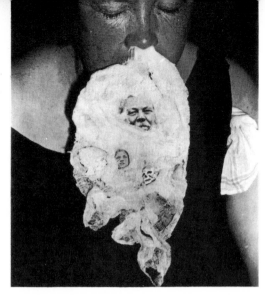

Left *Dr J.A. Hamilton, one of Winipeg's most respected physicians, used a wide angle lens to take this photograph of a materialisation seance on June 27 1932. Another of the cameras that he was using can be seen at the right (courtesy of Margaret Hamilton Bach).*

Right *An enlargement shows that the face of Sir Arthur Conan Doyle is materialising in the ectoplasm coming from the medium's nose (courtesy of Margaret Hamilton Bach).*

Edison and his team of research assistants seem to have spent several years on the development of such an electronic communication instrument but Edison was always extremely secretive about his research until it had been perfected and patented and no real details of this device were ever revealed. When being interviewed, however, he dropped hints of his progress on several occasions, saying, for example, 'Those in the spirit world reveal a very low energy output and, therefore, the instrument designed to be used for communication was super delicate and as fine and responsive as human inventiveness can make it'.

During another interview he stated that a new kind of energy valve, designed to receive and magnify low energy signals, was the heart of the machine and that he had been working on it for more than four years. On yet another occasion he is reported to have said, 'My plan is to give the psychic research workers an apparatus which will help them with their work, just as the optical experts have given the microscope to the medical world'. When Edison died in 1931 no trace of such an instrument was found but he was neither the first nor the last man to try and perfect such a device. Psychic instruments, designed to detect, amplify and store the psychic energies of both the living and the dead, have been made and described under many different names.

Until recently these psychic instruments and machines have only been able to amplify or extend the psychic talents of sensitives in the way that a simple megaphone will amplify and direct the human voice. This is only the first simple step and it will only be after much more research and development has been carried out that we will be able to record and reproduce psychic and supernormal phenomena in the way that an expensive high fidelity recorder can record and reproduce the human voice. The first step will be from the human sensitive to a machine which will interact with and create a physical record of the phenomena and that first step has already been taken by supernormal photography.

Other research into methods of recording and intensifying the physical effect of supernormal phenomena include improvements to simple instruments such as the pendulums and rods used by dowsers and the detecting apparatus like the rubbing pads used in the Heironymous machine and other radionic instruments.

Similar stroking of the rubbing pads of psionic apparatus can be used for other purposes too. In Czechoslovakia, Robert Pavlita, the inventor of a number of new manufacturing processes used in the textile industry, has turned his attention to psionics and has developed many different psychic energy amplifiers which work

A face is materialising right through the one-piece sack-like garment being worn by the medium Eva C.

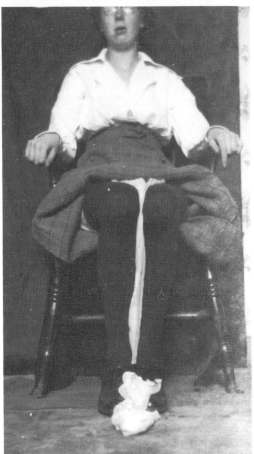

Ectoplasm exuding from the medium Kathleen Goligher. One of the large number of photographs taken by Dr J.W. Crawford often using several cameras simultaneously.

Right *Stephen Van Coops uses Polaroid film in his new aura camera. When he took this photograph of Cyril Permutt the colour grid in the background was obscured by the glowing aura from the author's head. In the original colour photograph this is golden with a red centre and Stephen claims that this shows the healing being extended to a patient at the time.*

Below *The table tilted paranormally by the tiny 4 ft 10 in tall medium, Mrs Poole, resists every effort by 6 ft 4 in Mr D.B. Macdonald to push it back to the floor (courtesy of Margaret Hamilton Bach).*

solely because of their shape and the materials which they are made of. Some of these psionic amplifiers are charged by stroking them, others by merely holding them and staring at special places in their designs. Their functions vary from killing insects to speeding up the growth of plants and there is even one which acts as a telepathy machine by pointing to the correct symbol on a Zenner Card that someone in another room is thinking of.

Orgone energy, discovered by Wilhelm Reich, is also now the subject of new intensive research. Reich concentrated this orgone energy in accumulating boxes made of alternate layers of wood and metal. He held that non-metallic substances, such as wood or stone, absorb orgone energy from the atmosphere and then release it slowly whilst metals absorb the orgone rapidly and release it rapidly so that, when placed next to each other, the metal will extract the orgone energy from the non-metal and expel it towards the side exposed to the air in a kind of psychic osmosis.

By arranging several metallic and non-metallic layers, folded into a box-like shape, the orgone is concentrated into the centre of the box and an orgone field extends for several inches in all directions around it. The presence of this energy field can be demonstrated by its effect on organic matter. Small pieces of meat placed on top of the orgone accumulator become preserved instead of going rancid and cut flowers last beyond any reasonable expectation.

Huna International, a non-profit research organisation based in Los Angeles, has produced a device based on this principle which they call Manabox. The name is derived from the Polynesian word 'mana' which means divine energy. Huna International claim that tests show that, like certain pyramid shapes, the Manabox produces a resonant energy field which will re-sharpen razor blades, improve the taste and bouquet of almost any cheap wine, rid badly brewed coffee of its bitterness and smooth and improve the taste of almost any kind of food or drink placed on it. Unlike the pyramid shapes, this effect is not dependent upon any special alignment with the Earth's magnetic or gravitational fields although it may interact to some extent with them.

The power of a Manabox seems to depend more on the number of dual layers of metallic and non-metallic materials, which Reich called 'folds', than upon its size

Left *John Mullins, founder of the famous firm John Mullins and Sons, Water Diviners and Engineers, of Bath.*

Above right *Cyril Permutt and Ian Cipin at Stonehenge, August 1982. The dowsing rod in the author's hands reacted violently to the fields of psychic energy around the stone circle (Philip Permutt).*

and it is suggested that this is in some way analogous to a voltaic pile. Some psychics claim that they can feel or sense the energy field produced by these orgone accumulators and interesting experiments are now being undertaken to see if this energy can be photographed.

This ability to detect orgone energy fields is akin to the sensitivity of dowsers to underground streams of water and deposits of mineral ores and the similar sensitivity of some people to magnetic fields. The fact that sensitive people can see the visual appearance of the magnetic aura, streaming from the poles of strong permanent magnets and from the finger tips of powerfully magnetic people, was discovered by Baron Carl von Reichenbach in Germany in the 1840s.

Even the possibility of this being correct was strongly denied by orthodox scientists until experiments in 1896 showed that the magnetic field of a bar magnet of 8,700 Gauss strength, held near to the temple, causes intense light sensations in complete darkness as well as in bright daylight. Even then the facts were not accepted until, in further experiments on the effects of magnetism on man in 1910, Silvanus P. Thompson, a British scientist, confirmed that a strong magnetic field caused a flickering visual sensation in the eyes.

These visual effects of magnetism are called the magnetic phosphene effect and further studies carried out in 1911 at Johns Hopkins University by Knight Dunlop, a leading American physiologist, provided further confirmation and showed that, whilst all the subjects saw these flickering lights and other visual effects when subjected to a strong magnetic field, in a low intensity magnetic field only a few sensitives saw them, once again confirming Reichenbach's original findings of some 60 years earlier.

More recent work by Horace B. Harlow at the Massachusetts Institute of Technology, using a magnet of 900 Gauss magnetic flux density, shows that moving the magnet makes the visual effects appear to alter and move about and that moving the head or blinking the eyes extends the length of time that these effects remain visible.

Although there has so far been no reasonable explanation for it this magnetic phosphene effect seems to be affected by both hypnosis and certain drugs and it has been shown that subjects under hypnosis, or in a state of mescalin intoxication, can often 'see' a static magnetic field by the visual flicker effect that it causes. It has been suggested that such a visual effect is behind the appearances of ghosts and that

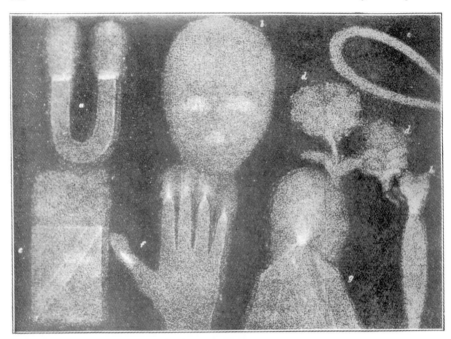

Above *Pictures of the aura from the fingertips of powerfully magnetic people and from magnetised objects made by M. Ansuchietz during experiments with Baron Karl von Reichenbach. From Le Fluide des Magnetiseurs by Baron Karl von Reichenbach circa 1840.*

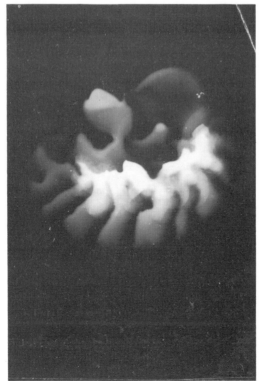

Left *'Astrophytum of Cerebellum'. Radionic photograph taken with the Delawarr camera for confirmation of radionic analysis of the disease (courtesy of the Delawarr Laboratories, Oxford).*

Above right *A typical seance room, the cabinet is formed by a curtain and two solid walls in the corner of a room.*

the poltergeist's activity of table turning and the other physcial manifestations of psychokinetic energy, both those attributed by Spiritualists to the discarnate personalities of the dead and those attributed by parapsychologists to the psyche of the living, are all directly or indirectly due to our interaction with the Earth's geomagnetic field.

Karl von Reichenbach told of successful experiments with table turning in a darkened room in which a small roller apparatus, designed by Faraday in June 1865, was placed under the hands of the sitters around the table so as to prevent them coming in to any contact with the table itself. He also suggested a small experimental test for psychokinesis whereby a small visiting card is balanced on the tip of the index finger of the right hand. With most people the card remains quite steady but with a few people it soon begins to move around in small jerky movements. If the card is placed on all five fingertips put together the movements are often more effective. Dowsers are amongst those who are more successful with this type of experiment, as are spiritual healers and mediums and the effect can often be enhanced by placing the subject in an hypnotic trance before the experiment commences.

Psychokinesis—the ability to move or control the movement of objects mentally, without touching them or influencing them physically in any way—is perhaps one of the most awe inspiring of the talents which are being investigated by the new science of parapsychology and it is the most easy to record photographically.

Spontaneous examples of psychokinesis are called poltergeist activity. Poltergeist is a German word that literally means noisy spirit and the activities which it covers include inexplicable movements of objects, their unexplained disappearance and reappearance and the non-physical production of knocking, rapping and other noises. It usually occurs in the presence or vicinity of adolescent youngsters, more often girls than boys, who are often emotionally disturbed. Occurring frequently enough to be subjected to thorough investigation, this paranormal power which flings household utensils and heavy items of furniture about in empty rooms has more recently also been found to affect electric lights and telephones.

The files of the Society for Psychical Research are full of the authenticated details of such cases and the services of both excorcists and psychiatrists have been used to help solve the problems which cause these poltergeist outbursts and the further problems which often occur. Indeed the approach of many excorcists seems to be that of a lay psychiatrist and it may be that professional help before the incident occurs is what is really needed.

Recurrent Spontaneous Psychokinesis (RSPK) is the name given to poltergeist activity by parapsychologists and, although it is perhaps a more descriptive and scientific name, the old term poltergeist is still very much in use. Psychokinesis is the division of parapsychology that deals with such examples of the action of the human mind or psyche on the physical world without the normal intervention of the muscles or body. Psychokinesis, the word is usually abbreviated to PK, has been solidly established through decades of experimental laboratory work, at first with dice and other small moving targets and latterly with electronic equipment and stationary objects.

Spontaneous outbreaks of poltergeist activity—the movement and throwing about of inanimate objects, sometimes small and sometimes large, pieces of furniture and equipment and the levitation of human beings—are more violent and powerful examples of PK whilst the extra images seen in many supernormal photographs seem to be the result of a more delicate manipulation of matter by the same talent.

Although paranormal photographs fall into two distinct categories, those which are the result of spontaneous phenomena and those which are the result of controlled investigations and experiments, both are impressed by the action of the human psyche either living or deceased. Because of this, many scientific investigators of the supernormal are becoming more and more convinced that the extra images are indeed recorded on these photographs by something akin to, if not part of, this wild talent or power to influence mentally physical objects that we call PK.

Over the last few decades more intense investigation of PK activities has been undertaken and they have been witnessed and recorded by several scientific observers. William G. Roll of the Psychical Research Foundation at Durham, North Carolina, and Dr J.G. Pratt have investigated several reported cases of poltergeist activity and reported on one outstanding example, 'The Miami Disturbances', in the *Journal of the American Society for Psychical Research*, Volume 65, pages 409-54, 1971.

Disturbances and breakages of stock at a wholesale novelty warehouse in Miami, Florida, commenced at the end of 1966, carried on for some time and, in January 1967, one of the owners, Mr Laubheim, reported them to the police department. Articles which were safely stored on shelves in the warehouse began falling and sometimes indeed leaping off shelves when no one was near them and the list of breakages became increasingly alarming. The incidents were witnessed and investigated by the police, the insurance company involved and several private individuals, as well as by Roll and Dr Pratt and a number of journalists and radio and television reporters.

The warehouse was a large room with two desks near the front, entrance shelves along one side, three stacks of shelves down the centre and two wrapping tables at

The young boy who was the focus of the poltergeist (see the author's paper 'The Bournemouth Poltergeist', Journal of the Society for Psychical Research 1983). (Photograph courtesy of David Haith and the Times Herald Newspapers, Dorset.)

the far end. The incidents, which included over 200 articles falling from the shelves to the floor, some of them flying through the air (the furthest one to a distance of 22 ft from the shelf) caused much damage and many breakages as these articles included beer mugs, glasses and boxes of fragile novelties. Special care was taken to ensure that none of the objects could have moved accidentally and often two or three were jammed together on shelves which were rigorously tested for firmness and stability, but the disturbances carried on for over three weeks.

Roll and Pratt painstakingly charted each incident and the position of everyone present at the time on a large floor plan of the warehouse and arranged selected objects on shelves in specially examined and watched parts of the room. Even these were seen to be moved but, regrettably, no photographic experiments were conducted. Their conclusion, that this spontaneous psychokinesis was centred around one of the young clerks employed in the warehouse, a 19-year-old Cuban refugee called Julio who was very emotionally upset and had family difficulties, was based on the fact that almost invariably the poltergeist activities only occurred when he was

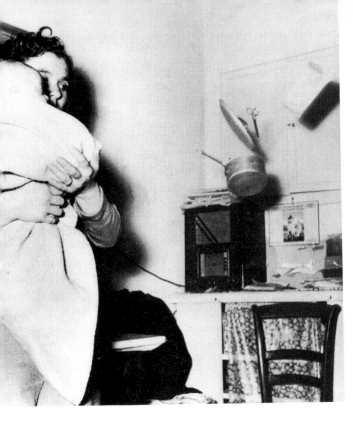

Gerrard Lestienne, photographer, and his colleague reporter Michel Agallet were sent by their newspaper Samedi Soir *to investigate this case of poltergeist activity. They examined the room, the furniture and utensils and found nothing. The only people they allowed in the room were 24-year-old Teresa Costa and her baby and a man from the village who sat in a corner. After an hour and a half they heard a knock and Lestienne released the camera shutter and captured this photograph showing a saucepan, its lid, a pair of scissors and a telegraph form flying through the air. He later secured other remarkable photographs of the phenomena that they witnessed (courtesy the Archives of the Bureau for the Investigation of Paranormal Photographs).*

present. This was confirmed when the activity ceased when Julio stopped working there at the end of the month.

Another similarly well investigated case of poltergeist activity was the Rosenheim poltergeist. Dr Hans Bender, an experienced parapsychologist, investigated this outbreak of poltergeist activity and made videotape recordings of a number of the phenomena. Mr Sigmund Adam, a lawyer in Rosenheim, Bavaria, complained to the utility companies concerned when fuses began to burn out, fluorescent lights switched on and off, light bulbs burst and his telephone continuously malfunctioned. Although the electrical system at the office was isolated by connecting it to a special emergency generator, inexplicable changes and strong, but irregular, deflections in the current were registered. The telephone engineers were just as puzzled when the telephones rang without cause and when one of them kept on ringing the local time enquiry number, 0119, sometimes several times a minute, 40 to 50 times without the dial moving at all.

Dr Hans Bender and the crew of the mobile laboratory which he used for his parapsychological research observed that the activity only occurred when one of the staff—19-year-old Annemarie Schabel—was in the office. Videotape recordings were made of paintings swinging around the hooks on which they were suspended and hanging ceiling lamps swinging after Annemarie as she walked through the hall.

Many other phenomena, ranging from a 400 lb filing cabinet moving away from the wall, drawers opening and shutting on their own, chandeliers swinging wildly and ornaments flying off the walls were also observed but all the activity ceased when Annemarie left. In this case, too, the incidents took place when Annemarie was emotionally disturbed. She was not happy with her work and in the late afternoon, when most of the mysterious telephone calls were made, she was desperately looking forward to going home.

The importance of these and similar cases is that at long last they were being subjected to a thorough scientific scrutiny and were being recorded as they occurred. All that is needed now is to obtain more photographic evidence showing, not only the visible effects of such phenomena but also, if possible, photographic records of the supernormal force or energy involved directly on the photographic emulsion. This will enable us to take the next step in understanding and controlling these supernormal powers for the benefit of mankinds.

The psychokinetic movement of objects and the allied Geller effect of supernormal metal bending have been demonstrated all over the world and I have photographs of such demonstrations of PK taking place in places ranging from Great Britain to Japan and from Russia to the United States of America.

One such series of photographs, showing the supernormal movements of objects, sent to me by Dr John Thomas Richards, is a record of the work of Dr Richards and his associates in the Society for Research on Rapport and Telekinesis, the SORRAT group who have conducted most of their experiments at Skyrim Farm near Columbia, Missouri, USA.

The group, founded by Dr John G. Neihardt in October 1961, usually has about a dozen members and these have included people with occupations as varied as an Air Force officer, anthropologist, artist, medium, parapsychologist, psychiatrist, sensitive and a teacher. Within a few months of starting their regular weekly meetings, small objects placed on the oak table that they sat around began making spasmodic jerking movements, cold spots were noticed and raps were heard coming from the table and other pieces of furniture in the room.

By the autumn of 1965, after careful and regular efforts, they found that they were able to levitate the table and when, in February 1966, they began to use a light metal snack tray instead of the heavy wooden table they found that the tray not only levitated clear of the floor but moved apparently of its own voliltion from under their hands and floated by itself to the ceiling. Dr Richards, who has kept a careful record of the experiments, reported that the tray has levitated to a height of 15 ft, has stayed aloft for as long as three minutes and has seemingly tap danced on the top of a parked car when the experiments were conducted out of doors.

Dr Richards told me that he and other members of the SORRAT group have used cameras, ranging from simple ones such as the Kodak Pony 620, Kodak 127 and Kodak Instamatic 126 to 35 mm cameras with special flash and filters for infra-red photography and that visiting photographers have used a variety of more expensive and sophisticated press cameras and Nikons, etc, to record the results of these experiments. This, of course, is the kind of photographic coverage that all research of this kind should have.

The SORRAT group have co-operated with many other American parapsychologists and have conducted experiments with Dr J.B. Rhine and other leading researchers in this field. Dr Rhine has suggested the use of sealed glass mini-laboratories to show that there is no possibility of fraud or trickery being the cause of the effects produced and W.E. Cox of the Foundation for Research on the Nature of Man and his assistant, Steve Calvin, have designed the Cox-Calvin RSPK Automatic Filming Device which does just that.

Target objects which might move paranormally are placed on electrical pressure switches or copper prongs so that the movement of any of them from their position sets off a solenoid arrangement which triggers two 100-Watt lamps set 2 ft away, a stop clock, an electric clock and a Bell & Howell spring-driven 8 mm cine camera

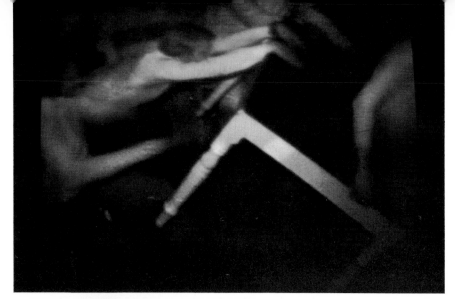

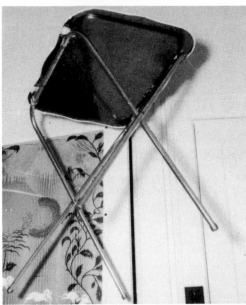

Above *Conducting their researches into psychokinesis in complete darkness this group of psychology degree students, led by K. Batcheldor a qualified psychologist, used an infra-red video camera to record the antics of their animated table on November 17 1978 (courtesy of K. Batcheldor).*

Left *Complete table levitations without contact have been achieved by SORRAT in their experiments at Skyrim Farm, Columbia, Missouri, USA.*

Below *Taken in complete darkness using an infra-red flash this photograph shows that the combined efforts of the group could not hold the table down (courtesy of K.T. Batcheldor).*

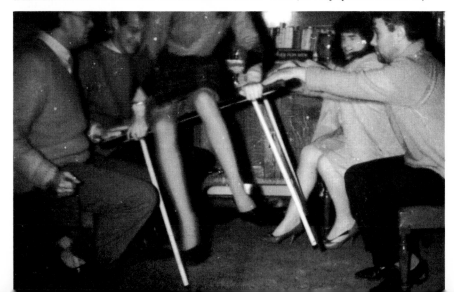

mounted so as to photograph all or any movements inside the miniature laboratory.

The camera uses ordinary Kodak indoor film and by July 1979 the group had obtained four reels of 8 mm motion pictures which include startling paranormal phenomena such as the psychokinetic movement of small objects, the swinging of two pendulums, the paranormal movement of a cube through a layer of coffee grounds and, on four occasions, the actual filming of an unsupported pen or pencil in the act of rapidly writing a coherent message.

W.E. Cox has built many mechanical and electromagnetic machines to demonstrate the forces involved in psychokinesis and this Cox-Calvin RSPK device, which allows an experiment to be set up wherever strong PK activity can be expected to occur and left to record and photograph the phenomena by itself, is a great device. During the SORRAT experiments the glass walls of the box are strapped, locked and sealed tightly to the wooden base and every security precaution is taken to prevent surreptitious entry. This air-tight container is placed in an isolation room, such as the concrete walled fruit cellar which can be securely locked, and then left with the machine running until a designated time when it is checked. If it has been triggered off, the lights and camera are then re-set. Further suggested improvements in this device include monitoring the entire area of the isolation room with a continuous videotape security system which would show if it had been tampered with in any way.

Dr Hans Bender, Director of the Freiburg Institute, who has investigated many outbreaks of poltergeist phenomena, including the famous Rosenheim case and several other cases of RSPK which have occurred in Germany since then, uses a Volkswagen minibus, both as a mobile laboratory and as transport for the still, cine and television cameras and other apparatus that he uses, whenever possible, to record the display of spontaneous phenomena.

Dr Bender has also used sealed boxes to make an airtight, impregnable, miniature laboratory in which it can be shown that the phenomena which occur could only have been produced supernormally using light responsive photoelectric cells to trigger still or cine cameras and videotape recorders when objects are materialised out of nowhere. He has further suggested that high frequency cameras, taking up to 10,000 frames per second, would be the ideal instruments to show how the materialisation of objects occurs.

The advantage of sealed miniature laboratories such as the Cox-Calvin RSPK device and Dr Bender's airtight photographic boxes is that they can be set up at a place where physical phenomena have been or are expected to occur without the need for the researchers to keep constant watch for the sudden outbreak of spontaneous supernormal phenomena. Spiritualists could make use of similar devices to support their contention that the supernormal phenomena that they produce are not dependant upon the intervention of a living medium or seance circle but are rather the outcome of the activities of the post mortem personalities of people who are no longer living.

Dr Richards, for instance, tells me: 'That what happens is a product of intelligence, and that the intelligence is not solely that of the human beings physically present, is strongly indicated by the results of our experiments. Consequently the advantages of the Cox-Calvin device should be obvious to Spiritualists and non-Spiritualists alike . . . it provides an absolutely fraud-proof environment in which no human beings need to be present for supernormal activity to occur'.

I know of many occasions when such a device would have provided invaluable

photographic evidence of supernormal phenomena which were only partially recorded when they occurred. An outstanding series of supernormal events has been documented by Pat Montandon, a well known American TV personality, in her book, *The Intruders*, published by Angus & Robertson (UK) Ltd. Pat was one of the West Coast of America's brightest society hostesses when her problems began in the mid-1960s. She had just moved into a beautiful apartment in an old house overlooking San Fransisco Bay and as at that time mysticism, gurus and meditation were becoming fashionable, she gave an 'astrology' party complete with crystal gazers and a palmist.

The party was a marvellous success with everybody having a good deal of fun until a Tarot reader, who had been invited to entertain the guests, became upset over some imagined slight. Losing his temper, he swept out of the party with his uninvited entourage and, turning around in the doorway, shrieked furious curses on the hostess and house alike.

Over the next two years Pat Montandon suffered an uncanny series of misfortunes, misfortunes she could only account for as emanating from some malevolent influence. Her apartment was repeatedly ransacked by burglars, ravaged by fire and invaded by periods of penetrating damp chills even though radiators were turned up too hot to be touched. Bizarre incident followed incident. Her car was smashed up several times, her personal life was blighted with repeated misfortunes and unpleasantness and her dog refused to stay in the house with her. Finally, after a culminating tragedy involved the uncanny death by fire of her closest friend, Pat called in psychic investigators and subsequently had the apartment exorcised.

The psychic investigators, Gerri Patton and Nick Nocerino of The Institute of Psychic and Hypnotic Science of Vallejo, California, finally sent her a voluminous report which agreed with her feelings about the evil influences that were at work. What these two had experienced confirmed her worst forebodings. 'Strong swaying motion, smells of blood and smoke, feelings of being immersed in very hot water, tumbling sensation and dizziness' were just a few of the sensations which they had felt whilst exploring and photographing the house, and the report contained 26

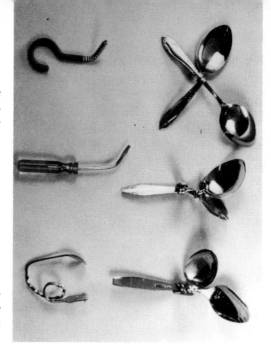

Left *Under close scrutiny Rudi Schneider successfully levitated the aluminium trumpet right up into the air.*

Right *Paranormal metal bending. Bottom right by a young girl Miss Tazuko Shima, others by Japanese teenage psychic Masuaki Kiyota (courtesy of Toshihiko Ichimura).*

8 in × 10 in black and white prints from the many rolls of films that Nick had exposed in the house.

He had used Eastman Kodak 400 ASA black and white film boosted to 600 ASA printed on Eastman Kodak Poly Contact 'N' resin-coated RC paper and Eastman Kodak 25 ASA colour slide film boosted as high as recommended, with some amazing supernormal results. These included the ghostly figure of a woman getting something out of a drawer, who certainly was not one of the three women present, bright patterns of light that look as if an area had been floodlit and deep purple stains with ghost-like blobs of white piercing them. Although at least 20 photographs were taken in the bedroom not one of them came out.

When I discussed these photographs with Pat Montandon she told me that they were so disturbing that she had insisted on taking the negatives to a laboratory in Santa Rosa to watch them being printed a second time so as to ensure that the supernormal images shown on the prints were not the result of dark room manipulation. She took elaborate precautions, recorded the entire proceeding and personally opened the sealed envelope containing the negatives and closely examined each one both before and after every printing.

Pat carefully watched every step of the proceedings but, despite these precautions, disturbing events continued to happen. Images of things that had not been visible in the house when the photographs were taken appeared on some of the prints and things that were not visible on the negatives appeared on others. The photograph of the enclosed porch area where Pat's dog had slept and where he had been subjected to such eerie attacks and torments that she had eventually been forced to give him away, shows a strange skull-like formation but it only became visible after the negative had been printed for a third time.

The ghostly figure of a woman reaching into a drawer appears in another photograph. When this photograph was taken there were only three women in the house, Pat Montandon, Gerri Patton (the psychic) and Phyllis Reilly who had been living there but was about to move away because she and her husband were also disturbed by the psychic phenomena. Although the features of the ghostly woman are indistinct, it was definitely not one of these three. Bursts of light, psychic energy

Left *Pat Montandon (courtesy of Angus & Robertson (UK) Ltd).*

Below *Who is this ghostly figure who seems to be searching for something in the drawer? It certainly was not any one of those present when the photograph was taken (courtesy of Pat Montandon).*

Below right *This photograph was taken from the top of the stairs, looking down into the foyer. There was such a pattern of light that it would appear the area had been floodlit. Yet the foyer had only a small chandelier, and was never a bright place at any time, and Nick Nocerino had not used any flashbulbs. The light was so strong near the newel post that it had virtually eaten into the silhouette of the upright. The caption to this photograph read: "Gerri Patton and I (Nick) at top of stairs feeling of plunging down, very strong, hard to control, almost went to jump into air and tumble down stairs, pushed feeling very strong". (Courtesy of Pat Montandon).*

and ghostly illuminations appear on many of the other prints although no flash or flood lighting had been used when the photographs were taken and on others the features of those present seem to change as though someone else was taking over their bodies.

I have examined many of these photographs myself and Pat has also shown them to many other parapsychologists, including Edgar Mitchell, the famous astronaut who became the director of the Institute of Noetic Sciences in Palo Alto. On examining the pictures, Mitchell said that a photograph might be the easiest way to prove the existence of psychic phenomena, but because it was so easy to distort photographs they are not accepted as hard proof. However, having investigated this case myself, I am of the opinion that these photographs, like so many other psychic photographs, are indeed genuine records of supernormal phenomena.

Many of the supernormal photographs that we have dealt with so far have been the results of deliberate experimental procedures designed to produce either physical phenomena that can be photographed or direct extra images on the photographic emulsion itself. There is, however, a large body of photographic evidence of the supernormal that is the result of spontaneous rather than deliberately produced phenomena and is as astounding in its quality and quantity as any other type of supernormal photography.

The Bureau for the Investigation of Paranormal Photographs, The Society for Psychical Research and many other similar organisations receive a steady stream of these spontaneously-produced supernormal photographs from members of the public, commercial photographers, professional portrait photographers and the press and the very diversity of their sources is in itself some guarantee of their authenticity.

When, for instance, Heather Buttery, a reporter on the *Hayes Gazette*, interviewed medium and spirit healer, Mrs Eve Hale, in January 1977, she was at first sceptical about the psychic photograph that showed a light, aura-like cloud over Mrs Hale's head in which can be seen the faces of her late father and grandmother. Heather's

scepticism soon disappeared, however, when her colleague, *Hayes Gazette* photographer Graham Bowles, processed the photograph he had taken during the interview showing Mrs Hale demonstrating the spiritual healing process. The photograph, taken by electronic flash and exposed for $\frac{1}{60}$ second at f8, shows a band of light streaming down across the picture which Graham Bowles said was completely inexplicable as it was not visible at the time and should not be on the photograph, but which Mrs Hale claims is a photograph of a spirit manifestation.

Another typical example was sent to me by Mrs Margaret Hawthorne, an attractive and intelligent young housewife who was on holiday with her husband in July 1977 when the photograph illustrated here was taken in the garden of May Cottage, Hunstanton Road, Titchwell, Norfolk. Mrs Hawthorn, who has been a Spiritualist since she was 17, told me that when she first arrived at May Cottage and entered the garden she sensed a presence that she did not like and felt most uncomfortable there. By the end of their stay, she and her husband were being disturbed by groans, bangs and a baby crying but although they searched the house and grounds thoroughly on several occasions they could not find any reasonable explanation for the phenomena other than the post mortem presence of a discarnate person.

What happens to us when we die is the question that keeps cropping up in the investigation of supernormal and psychic photographs. William G. Roll, director of the Psychical Research Foundation Inc, Durham, North Carolina, USA, and a founder member of the Parapsychological Association, a professional organisation of parapsychologists, originated the use of the word 'Theta' as a name for what is supposed to survive in a case of post mortem survival. This is derived from the Greek letter 'theta' and the Greek word 'thanatos' which means death.

It would seem to be these revolutionary aspects of the idea of post mortem survival which are the cause of the extremes to which critics of Spiritualism and psychical research are willing to go to in order to discredit the evidence and even to impugn the honesty of the researchers.

Modern parapsychological research, although mainly aimed in other directions, often produces evidence in support of the kind of human existence after death which is described and subscribed to by all the great world religions. Research into many cases of reincarnation, for instance, has shown positive results and the ability of telepathists to communicate ideas and images over long distances by some non-physical means adds substance to the great number of carefully investigated and well documented cases of communications and photographs that have been produced by or through the influence of discarnate entities.

I am often asked where one can hope to photograph supernormal phenomena and an obvious place is, of course, at meetings or seances where clairvoyants, mediums and sensitives are attempting to bring about supernormal phenomena. Although I have received evidence of clairvoyance at many meetings, photographs showing supernormal phenomena have only been taken at very few of them.

At one meeting at the Hendon Library, The Burroughs, Hendon, London, England, on October 24 1979, for instance, no extra images appeared on any of the many photographs that I took during the course of the evening although Ursula Roberts, the well-known clairvoyant who conducted the meeting, gave considerable

Opposite *Taken by J. Perry with a Zeiss Ikon camera at a seance at the house of Mr and Mrs B. Doust in 1980. Time exposure of about five minutes with lens fully open.*

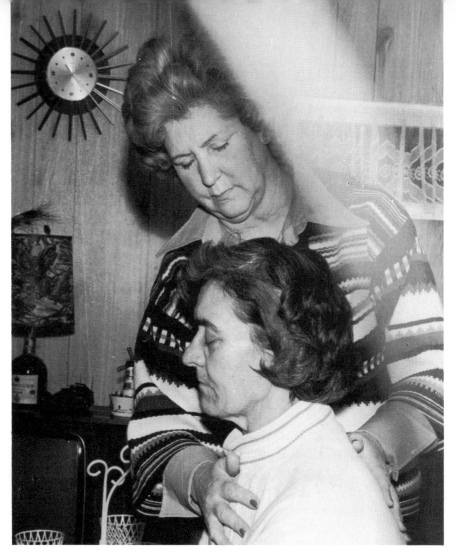

proof of her supernormal ability with messages from and descriptions of several people who were no longer living. These were acknowledged as being correct by the people who she was addressing, including the message given to me as coming from a short, tubby, rosy-cheeked, balding man of about 60 with very thin sandy hair who walked with short energetic steps. 'He,' she said, 'was carrying a set of books or ledgers under his arm and wanted to thank you for completing them for him and carrying on his work'. I was very impressed as this was an accurate description of my late stepfather and I did in fact carry on with his business, closing the accounts after he passed away.

An extra image did appear on a photograph which was taken by a *Cape Times* staff photographer in the Cape Town City Hall during a trance address given by Mrs Meurig Morris on Friday, June 28 1935. The ordinary negative film stock from the *Cape Times* photography department was used and it was developed in the ordinary way. Mrs Morris is shown on the platform with the chairman, Major General Sir Pomeroy Holland-Prior, and Mr Laurence Cowan who had sponsored her Sunday evening meetings at the Fortune Theatre in Covent Garden when Mrs Morris first appeared upon the London Spiritualist scene in 1931.

Left *Medium Eve Hale was tuning into her healing spirit when newspaper photographer Graham Bowles took this photograph in January 1977. He cannot explain the band of 'spirit light' in the top right section of the photograph which was exposed at $\frac{1}{60}$ second at f8 with electronic flash and processed with all his other news pictures.*

Right *'We seem to be covered by a whirling field of energy and a ball has appeared under my necklace although nothing was visible and there was no ball when this photograph was taken,'* Mrs Margaret Hawthorn, July 1977.

The ectoplasmic drapery seen hanging across the top of the stage was not visible in the City Hall when this photograph was taken. Although the *Cape Times* has taken hundreds of photographs in the City Hall, this was the first, and so far as I know the only—occasion on which a film has shown such markings.

Ectoplasmic materialisations have been photographed many times and a remarkable example is seen in the series of photographs of Reverend Keith Milton Rhinehart, the outstanding American medium who founded the Aquarian Foundation in Seattle, USA. These were taken during the International Spiritual Convention (October 31–November 7 1975) at the Olympic Hotel, Seattle, Washington, USA.

Reverend Rhinehart who was searched bodily by police officers Stephen Young and David Silverstein, sat in a seance cabinet which had been thoroughly examined and was guarded by the two police men who stood behind it. About 500 people from over 28 different countries watched and many took photographs in the seance room which was illuminated throughout by either ordinary white lights or by the light of 12 40-W lamps and was not at any time blacked out. In the photographs shown here ectoplasm can be seen pouring from Rhinehart's mouth and solar

Under police scrutiny and in the presence of witnesses the Rev Keith Milton Rhinehart produces an ectoplasmic materialisation (courtesy of Rev Keith Milton Rhinehart).

plexus until it forms a pool at his feet. One sitter, whose head clearly shows as she watches the amazing spectacle, illustrates how close the witnesses were stationed during the materialisations.

The mediumship of Keith Milton Rhinehart has been demonstrated and photographed on many other occasions too. In 1958 a committee of Japanese scientists made a thorough investigation of his mediumship, even going to the extent of having a special foolproof chair designed and built which they claimed precluded the possibility of physical interference with the phenomena which Reverend Rhinehart produced.

The manifestations that appeared during this series of seances and experiments were photographed with infra-red motion picture film and still pictures were also taken of them. One of these photographs shows a wide tape of ectoplasmic substance, about 4 or 5 ins wide, that flows from Rhinehart's solar plexus down to the floor and up on to the top of an adjacent table and forms a small three-fingered hand-like structure which is gripping a pencil and writing. At the end of the experiments this group of Japanese scientists, who included chemists, physicists and prominent researchers in other fields, stated that they were fully convinced of the honesty of both Rhinehart and the phenomena that were produced through his mediumship.

Reverend David Benson, the Spiritual leader of the Miami branch of the Aquarian Foundation Ltd, showed me a large album of photographs of the manifestations and other phenomena which have been taken at Rhinehart's seances, a number of which he and his wife, Janice, have witnessed personally and I have many more in my own files.

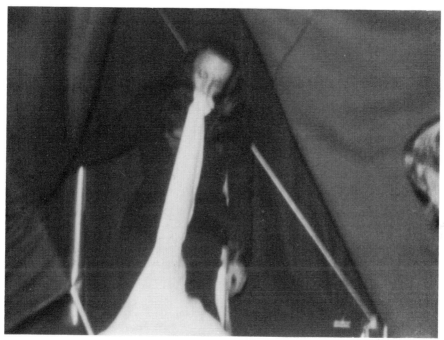

The silver cord flowing from the medium Rev Keith Milton Rhinehart to the fully formed materialisation can be clearly seen. The form then slowly dematerialised into a pool of ectoplasm on the floor. The seance room was illuminated at all times with either white light or 12 40-watt red lights and was photographed by many of those present with both regular and infra-red films (both photographs courtesy of Rev Keith Milton Rhinehart).

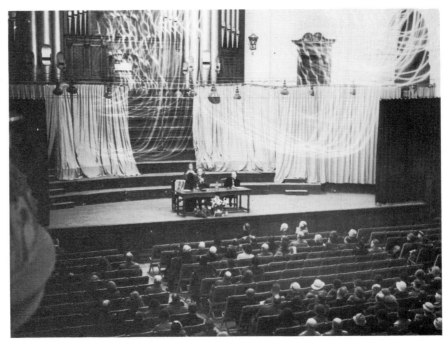

Above *Ectoplasmic drapery appeared on this photograph taken at a Mrs Meurig Morris appearance in South Africa by a* Cape Times *newspaper photographer in 1935.*

Right *Photograph taken in the Monastery Church of Teronimas, Lisbon, Portugal, on Thursday September 25 1934, at 11.30 am by Inga de Berries using a No 2 Brownie camera, time exposure of six seconds. The church was empty except for Captain J.V. Campbell who was standing behind the camera which was resting on the rail of side chapel facing the light. There was no window or light behind the camera and the rest of the roll of film was perfectly normal.*

Haunted houses provide excellent venues for taking supernormal and psychic photographs and old churches and ancient ruins are also good sites for such photographic experiments. Chingle Hall near Preston, Lancashire, is reputed to be the most haunted house in England and Mrs Margaret Howarth, the owner, who farms the surrounding land, told me about the many attempts that have been made by photographers to 'catch' one of the ghosts there.

The hall, which was built in 1260 in the form of a cross surrounded by a moat, is on the site of a Roman fort and, as soon as amateur historian Maurice Fitchett of Rochdale, entered the hall and started to compile the history of this haunted house, strange and unexplained incidents began occurring which eventually convinced him of the existence of at least one of the reputed ghosts. Maurice gave me details of some of these incidents which included ghostly footsteps following him around the house, doors opening and closing by themselves, door latches moving on their own and a constant feeling that someone or something was looking over his shoulder and watching his every movement.

Maurice, who is a down-to-earth technical representative, said that the ghost seemed to have an affinity with electricity as he often felt small electric shocks running up and down his legs when these incidents occurred and that on two

occasions a discharged flash gun, lying on a table, fired by itself, an action which was witnessed by Mrs Howarth, her sister, Miss Strickland and Mr Knowles, the family retainer.

The photograph of the ghost was taken not after hours of preparation and waiting but as one of a set of routine records of the entire hall. Its appearance on the print came as a shock as it had not been visible when the photograph had been taken and a thorough check showed that it could not be flare flash bounce or a reflection as on the next negative on the roll it had moved into the room and could be seen in front of the side of the armchair. Maurice, who kindly let me examine his original negatives prints and records, used a Zenith 3M camera and FP4 film giving an exposure of $\frac{1}{30}$ second at f5.6 with automatic flash to take these photographs.

Mrs Howarth has seen the apparition on several occasions. 'Sometimes,' she told me, 'it has the shape of a monk and is lit up brilliantly as if by hundreds of electric bulbs. Then it begins to fade as though the lights are being turned off until it finally vanishes', whilst at other times, 'It is just a tall dark figure', standing by her side. This monk-like figure has also been seen by Mr Knowles and several of the visitors to the Hall.

Granada Television and a number of newspapers, including the *Daily Mail*, have sent photographers to Chingle Hall to try to recreate Maurice Fitchett's photograph and several independent cameramen have also tried to photograph the haunting presence of the Hall but without success until New Zealander Michael Bingham spent five weeks there during April and May 1976. Armed with tape recorders, still and motion picture cameras and a history of the Hall's adventurous past, Michael sat in silence through the night, week after week, until his vigil finally paid off and he was able to show me what appears to be a photograph of a ghostly face peering through a window and, most exciting of all, a motion picture film of a spectre walking along a corridor and into the 'John Wall' room on the upper floor of the hall.

This was taken by setting up an 8 mm motion picture camera on a tripod with a 100-W lamp suspended beneath it. The tape recorder was left running at the same time and first the camera and then the light were switched on by remote control when the ghost's footsteps were heard in the hall. I have seen the film with the tape recorder running simultaneously and as we listened to the eerie footsteps we could clearly see the ghostly, luminous, apparently human, hooded figure moving along next to the left-hand wall of the corridor, walking towards the entrance of the John Wall room and moving to the right-hand side just before it gets to the door. The film has come out very very dark but one frame is unusual, there is much more light but it is only on one side of the frame and there is a white object at the bottom of the bed near the right-hand bottom corner of the picture.

Obtaining prints from this dimly lit 8 mm film have proved to be extremely difficult but one that we have managed to get shows a curtain-like shape obscuring the left-hand pane of the window and the white shape on the floor of the John Wall room which Michael believes are ectoplasmic structures. This print is taken from the section of film which shows the moving figure going up and down the corridor and the figure is only just visible about one third of the way from the right of the print.

A second photograph taken from the film running through a viewer/editor clearly shows the figure obscuring the doorway and I am trying to get a better print from a clip of this film that Michael Bingham kindly gave to me before he returned to New

Neville Davies of Waltham photographed by his wife beside King Richard's Well, Bosworth. The larger than life extra image of a man in mediaeval clothing is wearing the white rose of York on his breast. Bosworth Field was the scene of the battle in which King Richard III was killed.

Zealand. The many supernormal and psychic photographs that have been taken in churches and at other religious sites seem to give proof of the miraculous events that have occurred in these places, although I must confess to being singularly unsuccessful in finding any that have been taken in the Holy Land itself. Now that more and more people are visiting Israel and taking photographs at the Holy places, perhaps more will now be taken.

Visiting the old monastery church of Teronimus in Lisbon, Portugal, on Thursday, September 25 1934 at 11.30 am, for instance, Inga de Berries rested her No 2 Brownie box camera on the rail of a side chapel and, pointing it towards the open door, took a photograph of the church interior giving a time exposure of six seconds. The church was entirely empty except for her companion, Captain J.V. Campbell, who was standing behind the camera so there was no possibility of the extra image that shows on the negative having been made by someone who was only in the picture for part of the exposure. There was no window or light source behind the camera and the rest of the roll of film was perfectly normal.

On March 22 1959, Mrs Mabel Chinnery of Ipswich, Suffolk, visited the cemetery where her mother was buried and took some photographs of her grave. She used up the last exposure on the film by taking a photograph of her husband in the car. Mrs Chinnery says that, although when she took the photograph her husband was alone in the car, the photograph clearly shows her late mother sitting in the back seat in which she usually sat when they had taken her out for a drive (courtesy of Andrew Green).

My files contain many such examples of supernormal photographs taken in and around old churches and the ruins of old castles and the even earlier remains of megalithic monuments and the holy places of Druids are further fertile fields for photographic experimentation.

The factuality of psychic photographs, in many of which a deceased person's face is seen surrounded by a white cloud or haze, is shown by the many cases that have been reported of people actually seeing just such an effect themselves without the aid of camera or film. One such example is given by Louisa E. Rhine, one of the world's leading parapsychologists, in her book, *ESP In Life And Lab*, The Macmillan Company, New York, USA. In the second chapter she quotes an incident reported to her by a young woman who has had premonitions of danger and who refers to the following experience as the one that 'sticks in my memory'.

'I awoke suddenly and sat bolt upright in bed. There, above me and suspended in the darkness, was a face, normal size, surrounded by a white cloud or haze. The face was looking down at me and, of course, I was terrified. I blinked my eyes and felt the bed to make sure that I wasn't dreaming. The face then moved. It just floated down to me slowly, and I seemed to be hypnotised, staring into the eyes of it.

'I didn't say anything about it to my parents and would not be telling you now either if afterwards I hadn't heard my father in a hushed voice telling mother of his experience the night before! It was the same experience as mine! I listened to him describing the face just as I had seen it. Then I burst into the room and gushed out my own story.'

Large numbers of Spiritualist mediums have claimed to be able to see and to have established communications with people no longer living and produce much evidence to support their claims and the fact that most of this evidence is clearly of a circumstantial nature may well be due to imperfections inherent in the mediumship or the difficulty of communicating from the other side. Whatever it is that produces these phenomena may well be the causal factor in the production of photographs with the extra images of people who have passed from this life.

The truth must exist somewhere between the sceptical materialists who insist that they know all that there is to know and deny entirely the existence of the supernormal and those steeped in Spiritualist matters who, at the other extreme, claim that they can conjure up at will the spirits of saints and sinners, rulers and the ruled from Julius Caesar to President Lincoln.

Many people find that their experiences of the supernormal seem to be either sparked off by some intense emotional experience or alternatively the phenomena seem to be themselves the cause of an emotional upheaval in their lives. Spontaneous supernormal and psychic phenomena are often tinged with such emotional experiences and intense creative activity seems to be another type of emotional energy that can sometimes be inexplicably communicated between or shared by people. This is shown by the way that many great ideas and inventions have been discovered simultaneously and quite independently of each other by people who have never met and who were totally unaware of each other's existence until after they have announced their discoveries.

Certain functions of the mind such as clairvoyance, water divining, precognition and telepathy also seem to dissociate themselves from the central integrating functions of the brain which are our consciousness and ego. Recent developments and ideas on the nature of psychic and occult phenomena have given rise to the belief that there is indeed no supernormal and that the phenomena which seem to us to be supernormal today will be seen to have natural causes when we have a better understanding of supernormal and psychic phenomena.

Within our limited range of perception we are aware of many strange phenomena which appear to act from or come from somewhere outside our everyday space/time frame of reference and investigation of them seems almost invariably to lead us to the conclusion that some part of us does not die when our body ceases to function. Life is a pattern of energy which, like all energy, can be neither created nor destroyed, It can be changed from one form to another and can even be changed into matter and back from matter to energy again but the energy itself goes on for ever so, when we pass away from the physical world, the pattern of energy that is our eternal self remains intact.

Paranormal photography gives us visible proof that this is true and that our life is something infinitely more complex and beautiful than most people have ever suspected. It suggests that the physical, everyday part of our life—the here and now of living—is only a small part, an extract or crystalisation of our true selves, and that

this part evolves from and upon our physical death and dissolves back into the larger, total life form that is our real and true selves.

Sigmund Freud regarded human beings as systems of energy organised at different levels and his collaborator, Carl Gustav Jung, took this a stage further with the concept of the collective unconscious, the product of the entire evolution of the human race which we are all part of and which is part of each of us.

When we pass away from this world we do not die. The very word die is a misnomer. In the same way that the life in a chrysalis discards its worn out outer shell and emerges into the sunshine of a new existence so we shed the material trappings of this earthly life and release our true selves into the new world that is awaiting us. The truth of this simple fact which is the essence of most true religions only awaits the concerted investigation now made possible by modern science. That science has the resources for such a thorough investigation of the supernormal is beyond doubt. The tools of modern technology, from cameras to computers, which are all readily available for research into the supernormal, are instead being used for more and more esoteric research into the material world.

A vast outpouring of resources is going on at the laboratories of CERN, the *Centre European pour le Récherche Nucleaire* in Switzerland at Fermilab in the United States and at Novosibirsk in the Soviet Union. Here hundreds of the world's most distinguished nuclear physicists, assisted by thousands of technicians, have been using groups of six cameras in action simultaneously, each exposing miles of film and taking millions of photographs of cloud chamber reactions in their search for ever smaller and more elusive nuclear particles. Using enormous particle accelerators that combine electric magnetic and radio fields they increase the speed of the particles to almost the speed of light in research that is leading them more and more certainly to a point where physics and psychics overlap.

If only a small part of this vast outlay of trained manpower and material could be diverted to the investigation of the supernormal our entire concept of existence would change, but instead such investigation is mainly left in the hands of devoted dedicated amateurs and it is for this reason that the use of photography is so important in paranormal and psychic research. Photography places in our hands a simple instrument for recording the supernormal which is all around us and so producing the proof which will one day convince the doubters and persuade them to join with us in extending our knowledge and control of man's destiny.

The application of even a minimal amount of modern technology to psychic research by the use of electronic hardware to measure such things as the variations of electrical resistance of acupuncture points during psychic healing, or more conventionally by the use of items such as electroencephalographs, Faraday cages, and electronic temperature sensors during experiments, has led to some startling results, startling that is to those who thought that the use of such hardware would disprove the abundance of experimental evidence of supernormal photography.

In order to further investigations into supernormal photography, the Bureau for the Investigation of Supernormal Photographs has gathered a large amount of photographic evidence of the supernormal and the information collated so far has shown that supernormal photographs have been taken by a very varied assortment

Opposite *Two weeks after his death in October 1897 the face of Dean Vaughan and the initials D V appeared on the left-hand side of the entrance to Llandaff Cathedral to which he had been attached for a number of years.*

Field Marshal Sir Henry Wilson is transparent in this photograph taken by an Evening News *photographer as he unveiled the Great Eastern Railway War Memorial at Liverpool Street Station. One hour later he was assassinated by the IRA.*

of people ranging from teenagers and housewives to doctors, parapsychologists, professional photographers and TV personalities. The main difference is that whilst most people discard these photographs, professional photographers and parapsychologists tend to investigate and record the circumstances surrounding them.

We should all be aware of the fact that most people can and do produce psychic or supernormal photographs in suitable circumstances but unfortunately the photographs with extra images on them all are too often discarded or the negatives returned from processors as unprintable. Nevertheless there is now an enormous amount of photographic evidence that proves the existence of those wild talents that we call psychic or supernormal, even though much of the proof is too esoteric for the layman.

The straightforward and no nonsense methods outlined in this book are by contrast ones that anyone can use themselves with a minimum of equipment and expense, so to show the world that the supernormal can be recorded on photographs and that the supernormal does exist all round us here and now.

Index